TRISH CLARK

THE ROAD
TO
NALIN

If you want to save a village...
...build them a road!'

STEWART BRAND
AMERICAN ENVIRONMENTALIST. CREATOR AND
EDITOR OF THE WHOLE EARTH CATALOGUE

THE ROAD TO NALIN

A SMALL PROJECT...
A WORLD OF DIFFERENCE

BUILDING A **PROPER** ROAD TO AN IMPOVERISHED VILLAGE IN NORTHERN LAOS

Trish Clark

For Chanthy

Designed in Australia and published
by
High Adventure Publishing.com
Tumbulgum, 2490 Australia
© Trish Clark 2014
ISBN10   0-980784875
ISBN13   978-0980784879

Cover design :   Iain Finlay

Photographs :   Iain Finlay and Trish Clark

Maps: Google Maps

CONTENTS

CHAPTER		PAGE

INTRODUCTION

The Road to NaLin began as an adventure, turned into a love story and became something of a cautionary tale, though one with an immensely happy ending; all rolled together higgledy-piggledy by serendipitous accident.

It was a roller-coaster ride both physically and emotionally. With hindsight I understand it could not have been otherwise. Very occasionally it was like traveling in the fast lane on a straight highway while holding on to a tiger by the tail. Mostly it was a slow heavy trudge through the marshes while wearing heavy boots. The devil was in all the detail.

I have included something of these two aspects because now its done I realise, from the questions we have been asked, people want to hear about both.

In 2010 my husband, Iain Finlay and I, traveled the backcountry of northern Vietnam to cross into the wilds of Laos, that tiny country of six and a half million people, landlocked in the middle of south east Asia.

By journeying downriver in small boats we washed up in Luang Prabang, the former Royal Capital, for what we at first thought would be a stay of a couple of weeks. But we fell so immediately under its enchantment, the stay stretched into almost a year.

At first we set ourselves up to work on establishing our own independent Internet publishing company. Something we could have done anywhere we had access to the Internet. But what happened, very quickly and quite by chance, was that in addition to doing this, we also spent three hours a day giving unpaid English lessons to our landlady, a novice from our neighbouring temple and a young waiter.

Doing this gave us, again without any forward planning on our part, an entré into Lao life that would never have otherwise occurred. We became a part of the community around us; began to understand some of its many intricacies and levels of operation and to fall in love with the people and their culture.

We were invited to take part in local happenings. There were family meals, street parties, funerals; religious ceremonies, festivals, outings, a wedding and then the pivotal visit to a remote and impoverished village three hours by riverboat down the Mekong.

Here we know we must to do more than be just observers. At the time of our first visit NaLin, home to around three hundred people, almost all of them rice-farmers earning less than $3 a day, had no electricity. That came within the following year. But houses remain with no direct access to running water and though they have a primitive sewerage system the village is still without medical facilities and has just a very basic school for primary students only.

Worst of all, for almost six months of the year, during the annual wet season, the village had been all but cut off from the outside world when the one bush track in and out became virtually impassable. To get a sick child, an elderly person or a pregnant woman to a clinic, for a child to reach secondary school or just to bring produce to market, it was necessary to struggle through a several kilometer-long quagmire of knee-deep mud.

So in our naiveté we decided to attempt to help by doing something we knew absolutely nothing about. We would try to build the village a proper road with funds raised at home in Australia. That's where the cautionary tale kicks in! We learnt some hard, truths though we also experienced the revelation that help comes from unexpected sources: even a Communist government!

This story, a thank you letter to all those whose donations made building The Road possible, grew into being because I am an inveterate life-long diary keeper, note-taker and scribbler. I thought at one stage I was going to write a novel set in Laos, maybe I still will, but for now that idea has been subsumed into the telling of The Road.

It also contains road-trips inside Laos to the wonder-filled Elephant Festival and to the dark wartime memories of The Plain of Jars and the devastation of the Ho Chi Minh Trail in Xiengthong Province.

Through all this is threaded the story of a village boy who, 'bit by bit,' 'step by step' has followed his dream and become a knowledgeable and confident young man. In the process he has taught us a humbling amount about the world and ourselves.

This book is written for him, Chanthy Sisombuth.

Kopchai lai lai Chanthy.

NaLin village
relative to Muang
Nan and Luang
Prabang

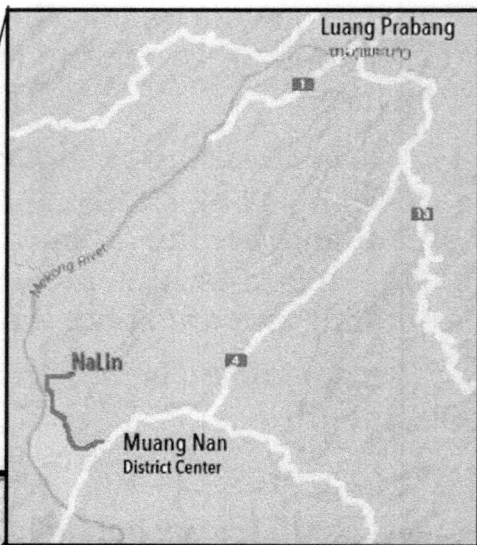

LAOS

Phujong Village

NaLin Village

Houayhe village

Hadsaikham
Village

16 Culvert
drains built on the road
to NaLin, Houayhe and
Phujong villages

The culverts shown on this map were installed as a second project nine months after the completion of the road work to NaLin, Houayhe and Phujong villages and are detailed in the Postscript on P. 297

Road to Muang Nan
district centre
(15 kms)

Luang Prabang

NaLin

Muang Nan
District Center

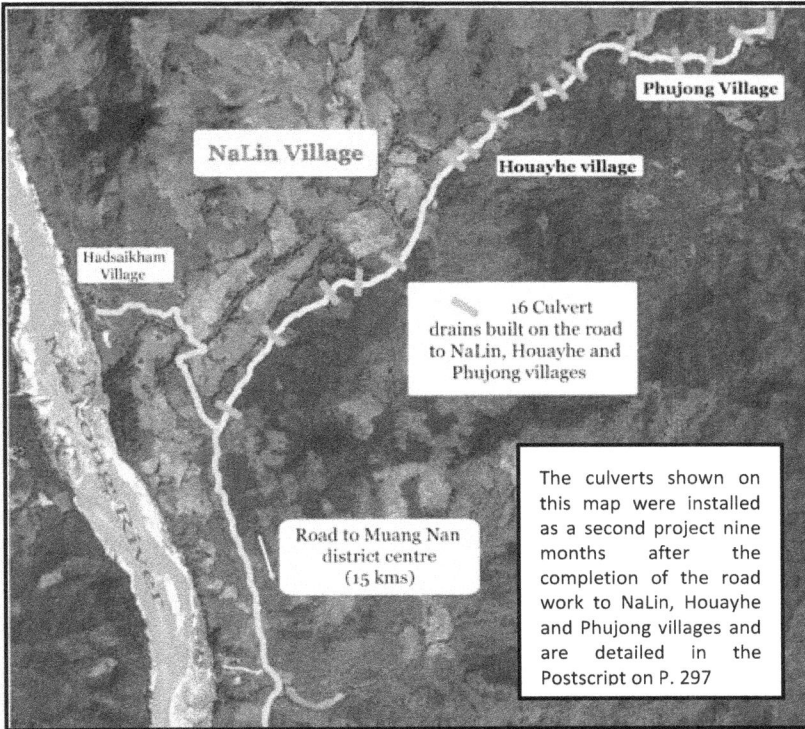

NaLin village relative to its neighbouring villages: Houayhe and Phujong

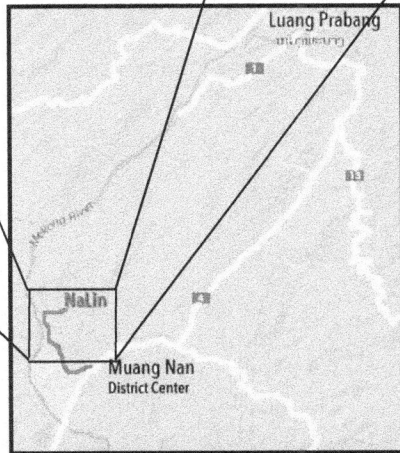

1

FINDING A NEST

It all started with a wedding.

Ms. Er married Mr. Vee and eight hundred guests, yes eight hundred! came to celebrate at a party held in the forecourt grounds of the local primary school in central Luang Prabang. This large open space faces out onto the main street that runs along the peninsula that is the lively heart of the former Royal Capital of what is now the Lao People's Democratic Republic, more familiarly known as Laos.

Luang Prabang is a World Heritage listed city an honour claimed for the most part because of the more than thirty Buddhist wats, or temples, that form an intrinsic part of the city's architecture and are home to at least three thousand orange-robed novices and monks. Their silent but always apparent presence creates an ineffable atmosphere.

In the grounds of the Royal Palace museum: Wat Mai

Monks at Wat Xiengthong

Why have we been invited to what, judging by the number of guests and also by how many of those had made long journeys to be here, could only be Luang Prabang's wedding of the year? Simply because we have struck up a friendship, a language-free friendship, with Ms. Er who owns the Khonkhai restaurant, which just happens to be the place we chose to eat on our very first night in town.

The Khonkhai, or Stone Chicken, appealed because its tables run along the paved parapet overlooking the Namkhan River; that's the smaller river at whose confluence with the mighty Mekong is the finger of land on which perches Luang Prabang with its thirty-three wats, or Buddhist temples. Khonkhai has white tablecloths and after the rigours of the twelve-hour bus trip, though covering a mere one hundred kilometers, bus through the newly opened border gate between northern Vietnam and northern Laos, followed by a two day small boat journey down the Namou river, we reckon we would benefit from the lift white tablecloths provides to our sometimes suburban souls!

We have come to Luang Prabang at the suggestion of an Australian friend, Robin Taylor, whom we had met when we were all Hanoi-based volunteers. Robin is now working in Vientiane for the highly contentious Mekong River Commission and her plan to take a ten-day break in Luang Prabang coincides with us, or rather me, finishing up in Hanoi after a month-long, somewhat demanding English Language Training course. We think that coming into Laos overland, through a more or less back door route will be a great slow-mo intro to the land of Laos, as well as a head-clearing exercise following too much brain use in Hanoi.

After rendezvousing with Robin at the Senesouk Hotel we spend a pleasurable week or so with her unwinding. We join the multitude of tourists, taking a tuk-tuk out to the Kwansi Waterfalls to swim in their blue waters; journey a couple of hours back up the Mekong by boat to Pak Ou caves to marvel over the hundreds of ancient Buddha figures sheltered there; pay visits to the museum of the once-Royal Palace, numerous beautiful wats and the great Night Market. In between these pleasures we cycle about to get a general feel for the place.

The result is a growing feeling that ten days here is not enough and by the time Robin has to leave to return to Vientiane we have a mind to look around in an effort to find somewhere we can stay on a more long-term basis.

We have decided to take back some of the power in our professional lives by establishing our own independent company, *High Adventure Publishing* to re-release, on Amazon and Kindle, our own previously published books, as well as new ones in the works. This is a big job that of course turns out to be even bigger than we anticipate. But all it requires is persistence and access to the Internet. So we begin the search for a place where we can set ourselves up. We want a place where we will be surrounded by beauty and peace.

We check out a few appealing guesthouses but it is obvious their busy-ness will preclude peace. We also cycle over to the other side of the Namkhan River to look at a whole two-storey house renting for less than $100 a week. But I sense we will spend too much time creating a nest for ourselves rather than getting on with our project. What we need is an instant nest.

On the way back into town we make a cold-call on what looks like a somewhat forlorn set of motel rooms, though set in attractive gardens. Here we strike gold by meeting the owner, a recent returnee from thirty years spent in the USA, who assures us her cousin, we had quickly discovered that in Luang Prabang everyone is a cousin to everyone else! has a place that she assures us would be just the spot. It is at the pointy end of the peninsula among the oldest

and best-known wats.

How right she is. Khoumxiengthong Guest House, close to the temple complex of Wat Xiengthong, is a traditional Lao style, large family house; white painted plasterboard set between dark timber uprights and with a tall roofline. On land behind this home and separated from it by a small garden and courtyard is a very recently constructed set of spacious rooms; three downstairs and another three above. As a bonus the rooms come with many subtle additions hand created by the artistic owner, Mr. Noi.

We negotiate a very good long-stay rental, to be paid in American dollars, for a simply perfect room, upstairs; large and rectangular in shape, with a high-raked ceiling, a king sized bed, a wardrobe and a bar fridge. There is also air conditioning and a ceiling fan with a separate small bathroom and shower. What more could one need?

Best of all is the fact that the door of this room opens onto a long, broad verandah, facing out into the tops of coconut palms and other tropical foliage.

Noi and wife Thiemchanh

Khoumxiengthong Guest House and our balcony

6

It will be here, we quickly realize, that we will be able to sit at a small table and work on our project; our two Macs linked to the Internet via Mr. Noi's wi-fi set up.

Our big room also has six full-wall-length, double-opening windows looking out onto more palm trees while the two at the far end embrace the courtyard of the big Sirimounkhoum Sayaram Wat, presenting an intimate view of the lives of the twenty or so novices living within these simple facilities. We have no inkling of how well we will come to know one of these novices and of the impact we will all have on each other.

We pay three months rent in advance, move in and begin our new lives.

2

THE WEDDING

Khonkhai Restaurant becomes a favourite spot for our evening meal. We gradually eat our way along through the riverside cafes, trying one place after another, usually managing to time our meal with the going down of the sun. This means we can ogle the tremendous, still beauty of the great ball of fire disappearing into the illusionary calm of the Mekong. But at least once a week we return to the Stone Chicken and the delicious home cooking of Ms. Er.

She invariably greets us with her wide-welcome smile, making a mental note of our meal choice. She then crosses the not too busy road that runs between the river and the smaller cross street that goes up a slight rise and in the middle of which she lives with her large extended family. All meals are prepared on the floor here; Ms. Er adjusting her sinh to squat down on her haunches so as to chop and pound, fry and bake on tiny cook tops fired by charcoal brickets.

Gradually, perhaps as the family realize we are not the more usual four-day-tourists, it becomes acceptable for us to hangout here as part of the scenery, along with the array of constantly under-repair family motorbikes, the air-drying pieces of indeterminate carcasses and the buffalo blood sausages, of which more, unfortunately, later.

Ms. Er's close family members are easily distinguishable from more distant relatives and neighbours because they all share the same physique. They are, especially by Lao standards, big, wide-bodied and square-shouldered. Ms. Er is by far the smallest, by comparison petite even.

Occasionally we spot, amongst all this outsized flesh, a man who is tall and thin to the point of gauntness with markedly different facial features. We recognize these, from having lived in Hanoi, as probably being Vietnamese. This is Mr. Vee.

Mr.Vee comes from the south, from Savannakhet and is an electrician, or a linesman, or has his own electrical company: very hard to get the fine detail about this without the language. What is not difficult to get is that he and Ms. Er are to be married.

The marriage invite is quite smicko, all red and gold, embossed with the beautiful flowing Lao script. Knowing there must be a specific etiquette involved: what to take as a gift and how to present it, what to wear, and whether to be early, late or even on time, we show it to our landlord, Noi and ask his advice.

Noi means Little Brother so naturally there are hundreds of Nois in Luang Prabang and no doubt thousands spread across Laos. 'Our Noi' was yet another case of us having serendipitously fallen on our feet.

You may have spotted in the last chapter's description of our accommodation, that something is missing in our room. Yes that's right; no cooking facilities. Whoa! How great is that! It means eating out! We do keep some nibblies in the fridge for midday top ups. But for breakfast, which Noi is happy to serve us in the courtyard downstairs, we often choose instead to go either French style to Le Banetton: baguettes, pain chocolate or croissants; home-style at Morning Glory (sadly since closed): fruit, muesli, fried eggs or Lao-style at the neighbouring well-patronised noodle shop.

For dinner: the choice is endless. But the Stone Chicken establishes itself as a favourite because of Ms. Er's cooking: nothing outshines her fish laap and green papaya salad. But also because of her warm embracing nature and the way we are accepted by her family.

Which brings me back to the wedding, when life for us made an unexpected and large diversion.

The wedding, Noi explains, would involve daylong celebrations. First up is an event at the home of Ms. Er that will take place some time in the morning. Actual times and what exactly would happen at this event remain somewhat imprecise.

We decide to check out the situation and on our

early morning cycle, we go by the bottom of Ms. Er's small connecting street and find the whole throughway is filled with chairs and tables, the entire street canopied.

The entrance to Ms. Er's family home has been transformed by being hung about with brightly coloured Buddha flags. The forecourt is crowded with women squatting down on their haunches in their work-sarongs around numberless oversized aluminium bowls, kneading, chopping, slicing and pounding as they prepare vast quantities of food. They chat and laughingly wave at us to come join in.

A few hours later when we do return a young man comes out of the crowd that has developed and gives us to understand he has been designated to take care of us. How's that for hospitality.

The prancing dragon

To the sounds of gongs and cymbals accompanied by laughter and shouts around the corner, at the main road end of the laneway, there now comes a prancing dragon.

Red and golden yellow it is, with an open mouth rimmed with red fur and outsized bulbous eyes. Following behind the dragon, accompanied by even more gongs and cymbals played with gusto by men who are obviously enjoying their role in all of this, is a tall man made all the more thin by his ill-fitting 19th century Lao kingly costume from which his scrawny neck appears. Ah ha! It is the gaunt neck that reveals his identity! This is Mr. Vee!

At the entrance to Ms. Er's home the dragon halts in front of an ironwork gate we have never noticed before, because it has always been open. Now, symbolically, it is shut.

As the gates open the dragon and Mr. Vee are welcomed by Ms. Er's family and Ms. Er herself who is resplendent in a luscious golden top and green sinh. We catch a glimpse of a row of Buddhist monks seated quietly patient inside on the floor of the main room. The ceremony will be a private affair.

Miss Er and Mr. Vee

12

The young man, who has remained close by us throughout all this excitement, lets us know the wedding party proper will happen that evening, in the fore-court of the primary school on the main street. Timing is flexible but he suggests some time between 6.30pm and 7.30pm.

When we ask him about a gift he suggests putting a US$20 bill in a red envelope. It is the straightforward and open manner with which he makes this suggestion that sets the tone for our future relationship. Not that we realize this at the time.

The line-up, when we join it at 7pm, stretches for some hundred or so metres out into the main street of Luang Prabang and along the low wall around the big primary school in the centre of town.

The event has taken over the entire open area in front of the school. In the blaze of neon light that floods the forecourt we can see rows of long tables set with linen, cutlery, glassware, bottles of scotch and an abundance of flowers. There is already a milling crowd of people smiling and chatting animatedly.

Mr. Vee has changed into a well-cut heavy white silk suit. Ms. Er's is a resplendent apparition in a red silk top, surprisingly revealing one bare shoulder and a matching sinh both lavishly decorated with golden thread. Her hair is pulled up high and wrapped around a hairpiece. Her whole person seems a shimmer of jewelry and her face,

At the wedding

particularly her eyes, are spectacularly made-up. We hardly recognise the hard-working cook we have come to know.

We make our nops, placing our hands, palm against palm, high on our brows and lowering our heads; a gesture banned by the Communist Party when they came to power in 1975 as a symbol of subservience, but as they soon found, a social greeting impossible to eradicate.

Our red envelope joins the scores of others filling a large heart-shaped bowl on a side table and we are guided to our table by the young man from the morning who now appears as if by magic at our side...and who seems somehow familiar.

He seats us at a front table from where we have a good view of proceedings and we quickly realise we are the only truly *falang,* or foreign guests at the wedding. There are a handful, perhaps six, other foreigners but they all appear to be the married partners of Lao women. And I mean married. As we are to learn over the following months it is not just frowned upon but actually illegal for a foreigner, man or woman, to have sexual relations with a Lao national unless they are married.

Naturally, men and women being what we are, these stipulations are not always met. But these laws do set the general tenor of the society. Laos is not Thailand: a fact about which the Lao are happy to elaborate. Openly casual sexual entanglements are simply frowned upon and we are to hear many stories of the legal and social hurdles faced by foreign men, these stories were always about men rather than women, who wanted to pursue a friendship into a marriage. One result is that you knew when you met, or just looked at a Lao/foreigner couple that a lot of work had gone into making this a solid happening.

Equally apparent is that these wives are not from Luang Prabang, where modesty demands women wear their sinh only a tad above their ankles. The elegant wrap around skirts of these other wedding guests, though still decorated with traditional bands of heavy embroidery, reveal their calves. One or two even have the courage to brave the stares of local women and wear western style dresses. They must be from Vientiane the frowns accuse: that comparatively brash capital city just under four hundred kilometres to the south, because, well, you know, that's how things are in the capital. They even marry *falangs*.

Food is served and I am congratulating myself on managing to avoid consuming the small cubes of jellied buffalo blood, a great and apparently expensive delicacy, when we are also presented with buffalo blood sausages. To again refuse would have caused offence. Fortunately the music starts up and people around us move to join in the dance.

The music is a mix of live and recorded sounds and a blend of traditional and western plus westernized traditional and traditionalized western. It has no beginning and no end.

The dance, our appointed guide tells us, is called the *lam wong* or circle performance, which says it all. Individuals dance in circles while at the same time dancing in circles around each other. No touching. Simultaneously the whole group dances in a big circle. This circling is done very slowly and all the time fingers and hands are elegantly twirled.

Falangs attempting this look nothing short of ridiculous. The Lao, men and women, move languorously and with elegant style. The women's fitted tops and straight-line ankle-length sinhs make impossible anything more extravagant. Landlord Noi gallantly moves in to partner me, his innate sinuosity showing up my attempts as even more stolid. Iain does little better partnering Noi's wife

Thiemchanh.

It is somewhat of a relief to see that it is not just us who are awkward with the dancing. There are several tables at which are seated comparatively portly Lao men wearing western suits and ties and who are accompanied by somewhat over-dressed, over-jeweled Lao women. From the reverential manner with which they are approached and spoken to by other guests these are quite apparently Luang Prabang's A-listers. They are here because they add political clout or other forms of status to the event but they make for less than dashing figures on the playground/dance-floor. Their presence makes it apparent that this is not just any old wedding.

Back at our table, the Beer Lao and home brewed *lao-lao,* which is rotgut almost pure alcohol, are going down a treat with our fellow diners, with whom the best communication possible is smiles and nods.

Finally we get our young guide's name and a bit about him. He is Chanthy Sisombuth and he tells us he has worked as a waiter in Ms. Er's restaurant for some little time. Ah! Now we realize why his face seemed familiar. We learn that he comes from a small village about three hours down the Mekong. His parents are both rice farmers, his elder brother works on the buses that ply the road between Vientiane and Luang Prabang while his younger sister is still at high school. He also tells us he is studying English at a non-government college.

It takes a long time to get all this basic information sorted out, what with lack of a language in common and the sound levels of the music. But despite these impediments what is completely evident is that Chanthy is bright and focused.

The food and drink keep coming and we sit back to enjoy the spectacle of the non-stop circling, hand-undulating, body-shimmering dance.

Ms. Er and Mr. Vee, doing the rounds of each guest table, eventually find their way to us. With the help of Chanthy's translation, we manage some polite generalities, raise a glass in a toast, then they are on their way to the next table as the music, dancing and eating continues.

Thankfully, for us perennial early-nighters, Luang Prabang shuts down early. So a little after 10:00 pm we bid our newly acquired young friend good night and walk back the short distance to Khoumxiengthong Guest house. But before we slip into sleep I suggest, 'Perhaps on our ride tomorrow morning we should cycle passed Ms. Er's restaurant and ask Chanthy if he would like us to give him some help with his English.'

Mmmm,' Iain murmurs, all but asleep.

And so the adventure begins.

3

ELEPHANT FESTIVAL

Very shortly after the unrecognised-as-such life-changing event of the big wedding we take a boat journey for an hour and a half back up the Mekong towards the Thai border in order to travel a short distance inland to a village called Hongsa to wallow in the Elephantasia Festival.

The elephants on parade

The thinking behind this four-day-long event is the raising of consciousness about the plight of elephants in Thailand, Cambodia and most specifically Laos where they are in danger of becoming extinct through cruel overwork and neglect. This in the country known in former times as The Land of a Million Elephants and where a three-headed elephant beneath a Golden Parasol, features as the national emblem

The organizers hope the festival will settle into being an annual gala celebration. This is only its fourth year of operation so not surprisingly there are still quite a number of hiccoughs with which to contend. A couple of these: the water levels in the Mekong and the stupendous heat are way beyond any human control. Perhaps the same also applies to the 10,000 Lao and Thai, the 300 or so foreign visitors and perhaps even to the thirty plus elephants too.

But it is worth coping with the heat, the dust, the hard floor sleeping and the noise. Everything uncomfortable fades to insignificance. In some inexplicable comparison, living around the elephants is like swimming with wild dolphins!

The huge crowds hanging out in the jungle, drinking *lao-lao*, the Lao wearing their best gear and everyone dancing, singing, and admiring these huge beautiful beasts as they work and parade, eat and poop. The entire human mob feels honoured by their presence. Everything about them is so awe-inspiring.

Those tree-trunk-like, seemingly foot-less legs, the huge bulk of their bodies, the way they kneel like us and unlike dogs or cats, with their forearms forward, their neat thick toenails, their swishing tails that they can stiffen or arch at will and most amazing of all their proboscis like trunks, with the tiny sensitive wiggly bit on the very end. There is also their aura of ancient-ness. It is all so very different than experiencing them in a park, even South Africa's Kruger, though these Lao counterparts are of course a more petite version of their African cousins.

I just love jogging to keep up with them, because they certainly get up a pace, admiring their controlled bulk, their immense contained strength, all dressed up, painted, brightly caparisoned, topped with howdahs and mahouts.

I yearn to have the language to find out from these men how they feel about making a lifetime commitment to a member of another species, which all mahouts do and how that affects the relationships these men have with other members of their own species. The mahouts train from their early teens and once bonded with a young elephant, usually about the same age as themselves, live with them 'til death do us part'. Fascinating food for thought.

We watch the animals frolic in the river, obviously enjoying themselves enormously. And why wouldn't they. It must be such a relief for them to be able to take all that great weight off their feet.

We admire the ease with which they manhandle and haul about great piles of logs and the delicacy with which they sniff at proffered bananas.

We join other hushed spectators at a basi ceremony in which the monks give blessings to the animals and their mahouts and in which they are all, monks and elephants, joined together by one long basi cotton thread.

Elephants kneel and then line up for monks' blessings

We have such a good time in my idea of heaven. But in the three days we are there the Mekong has apparently dropped so dramatically we are informed that our trip up by river has become impossible to repeat as a return journey back down to Luang Prabang.

Falang ignorance, mixed with that ludicrous western belief that we can do anything, leads us at first, to a degree of disbelief and questioning of the validity of the news. Embarrassing. But after much asking around we do finally come to understand that Me Kong, Mother River, is no longer safe to travel on because of suddenly emergent shoals and shallows. We accept that we will have to find an alternative form of transport back to Luang Prabang. A several hundred kilometer overland detour, all by open backed trucks, emerges as the only alternative

On the advice of locals and with no idea of what if anything we would find there, we cram into the back of an already over-crowded four-wheel drive pickup that takes off across the surrounding jungle-clad passes towards

On the back roads of Laos

the provincial capital of Xainyaburi.

What I most recall from that four-hour dusty, bumpy journey is the sprinkling of large, waxy-looking, white blossoms throughout the tropical foliage. These proliferate across the seemingly endless mountains that stretch range after range into a distant blue horizon. But such mountainous beauty comes at a price, as it means that only six percent or even less of the land in Laos is cultivable.

In drab, seemingly unpopulated, Xainyaburi, the one person hanging about on the otherwise empty and un-surfaced main street turns out to have just returned from living in Melbourne for twenty years! Howzat! With distinctive Aussie gestures and slang he suggests we ask for a lift from a mate of his who has a small truck with which he does the run into Luang Prabang when the need arises.

In a further stroke of good fortune it eventuates that this mate is just about to embark on one such run, transporting an enormously heavy, solid teak table, plus a set of eight large dining chairs with ornately carved backs and arms. All of these he has roped into the large tray back of his truck. There is room, just, for us to squeeze in alongside. Fortunately the tray-top has a solid awning so there will be some protection from the blistering sun.

A reasonable fee is negotiated to the delight of the driver and his teenaged cousin for whom this is quite apparently an unanticipated bonus and we once more hit the bumps and dust of what is preposterously named a National Route.

Experience has honed us into being pretty good at this sort of rough travel. We always carry a few cheer-us-up nibblies; dried fruit, salted crackers, sardines and of course water. So we are not too anxious when told that the journey could take five, six hours or more. When conversation lags Iain has his puzzle book and I have my alpha state into which we can happily sink independently, while the track, for this is a National Route only in name, unwinds through the tropical vegetation and passes small villages.

Iain checks the tie-downs on the furniture, relieved that it appears securely roped; being run over by one of those massive chairs, let alone the table, would be a total crusher.

Occasionally we overtake a hunter, armed with an ancient rifle, a lasso and a woven carry-basket. Frequently too-small boys accompany these men. We also pass women, accompanied by too-small girls, carrying heroic loads of water, filled from small roadside waterfalls, in assorted plastic containers.

There is too the constant danger from unrestrained animals, dogs mostly, but also cockerels and hens. Not that I believe the driver would risk his load by swerving to spare the life of such small animals. Though perhaps the few buffalo we pass, being led by a nose-ring on a rope held by the owner, might give him pause for thought.

On and on. On and on. Hours of eating dust. More hours of jarring ruts. Every now and again we move our positions on the rim of the tray so as to relieve muscles and stay, as much as possible, out of the sun.

While there is still daylight we do drive through a sizeable settlement of established housing set up well back from the track. Over a year later, when scouring maps, we realize this is the district center of Muang Nan that, by that time had become so important in our lives. But on this first sighting, even if we had been told the name, it would have meant nothing to us.

In quick succession dusk is chased away by dark. The truck's headlights wanly illuminate the yellow eyes of animals and the trudging bodies of people of all ages continuing to go about their necessary chores.

There is a sudden swerving motion that brings both us to full alert. The driver brakes hard, a young woman appears as the passenger window is wound down, words are exchanged, money handed over and a small furry body, not yet quite dead, is grabbed. We take off again. Through the cabin's back window we can see the men talking animatedly as the passenger holds up the creature for inspection; about half the size of an adult koala, grey-furred and more than likely from an endangered species. They look pleased with their purchase. The teenager gives the wild animal one last fatal blow to the head and throws it under his feet.

Shortly after that in-your-face incident we happily reach a tee-junction, turn left and hit the tarmac. Within an hour of comparatively almost pleasurable travel, we are clambering down outside Khoumxiengthong Guest House, being greeted by an astounded Noi. Only when we see ourselves in the mirror of our bathroom do we appreciate the reason for his reaction. Covered in dust we look like ghosts and for the Lao ghosts are a real terror, especially when they smile.

4

THREE STUDENTS

Within less than a month we have not only one, not two, but three, 'English language students'. I carefully put that description in quotes because I don't want anyone to think, especially not any of our friends who are real teachers, that I imagine myself to be an English language teacher. It takes a helluva lot more than the one-month intensive CELTA course I had just completed in Hanoi to be able to accurately describe yourself as a teacher.

CELTA is the acronym for a Certificate in English Language Teaching to Adult speakers of other languages run by England's Cambridge University. It is an initial qualification for people with little or, as in my case, no previous teaching experience. It is one of the most widely taken qualifications of its kind and as anyone who has taken it will assure you, its tough.

Of the eleven other people, from around the

world, with whom I share classes in Hanoi one dropped out after ten days and another talked of dropping out from a high balcony and required calming down.

My decision to do the CELTA was a form of very late-onset mid-life crisis. The most concise reason I could give for deciding to go for it was a desire to 'do something useful.' Right!

So I save up my pennies and pay for the course. We pack away everything and I mean EVERYTHING from our house because, the letting agent assures us, 'no one wants to rent a furnished place.' Supported by my extraordinarily tolerant partner, we leave home on an open-ended journey that starts in Hanoi because that is where I had chosen to do the course.

A big part of the decision to do it there is that we had previously spent eighteen months working in Hanoi as volunteers with Radio The Voice of Vietnam. We feel at home there and will be away from the distractions of our real home. Fortuitously we had a 'home' in Hanoi, with Rebecca Hales, a fellow former volunteer and friend, who generously offers to have us stay with her for the month I was studying. The added plus is that Rebecca is a teacher: a more than real teacher.

I complete the course and pass but only because of the huge support of Rebecca and Iain. By that time I am at bursting point. I sleep for long, long recuperative amounts of time and when Robin Taylor's suggestion that we join her for a break in Luang Prabang arrives by email, we think; good one.

The idea is to give myself time to settle down by doing some tough travel, always very grounding and decide then what to do and where to go from there.

As it happens the decision was all but made for us.

Chanthy is so very obviously pleased to be asked if he would like some English language coaching. There is no hesitation, no game playing. He simply accepts our offer as if it was as natural for us to offer as it was for him to accept. It is my first lesson, with many, many more to follow, in giving and accepting with grace. We arrange that he will come to Khoumxiengthong Guest House in late afternoon after he finishes his day shift as a waiter at Khonkhai.

The next step for the two of us, Iain was integral to all this from day one, is to visit *My Library*. This one person NGO run by an excellent American woman, Carol Kresge, occupies a small two-storey space only one laneway back from the Mekong River. The place is perpetually crowded with Lao, almost all of them young men. Many have the distinctive round, flat, brown-skinned features of the Hmong people. The entrance area is always crammed with bicycles and plastic sandals, kicked off and left there by the visitors who are attracted by the free use of teaching resources, books, DVDs and personal computers.

My Library has since moved to premises near *Utopia*, the well-known restaurant/bar on the other side of town overlooking the Nam Khan river.

Here at last my CELTA trials come in useful. I could honestly present myself as a would-be teacher of English and feel only a little intimidated when Carol gives me a run-down on what books were what and where to look for books at the correct instruction level to meet Chanthy's needs. I have talked the talk now I am going to have to walk the walk and I find I am less intimidated than I would have been without that dratted certificate.

Carol just takes it for granted that I know what I am doing. How often life works like that. Let's face it, have you ever asked to see an airline pilot's certification before settling in with 350 other souls to put your life in her/his hands?

The books are ones Carol has imported, many from English language educational institutions and publishers in Thailand. *Landmark* is one such outfit that sticks in my mind. Though as I scoured through them over the following months, they were all redolent with the same embarrassing unrealities that I had found so offensive in my CELTA class. There is a market, a big market, for books to teach English that is relevant to the lives of real people in various underdeveloped parts of the world. Want a project?

I borrow three books I hope will capture Chanthy's interest as well as stretch his knowledge base. That afternoon he arrives, five minutes before the appointed time, a habit he sticks to. If he is going to be delayed or unable to keep the appointment he always telephones.

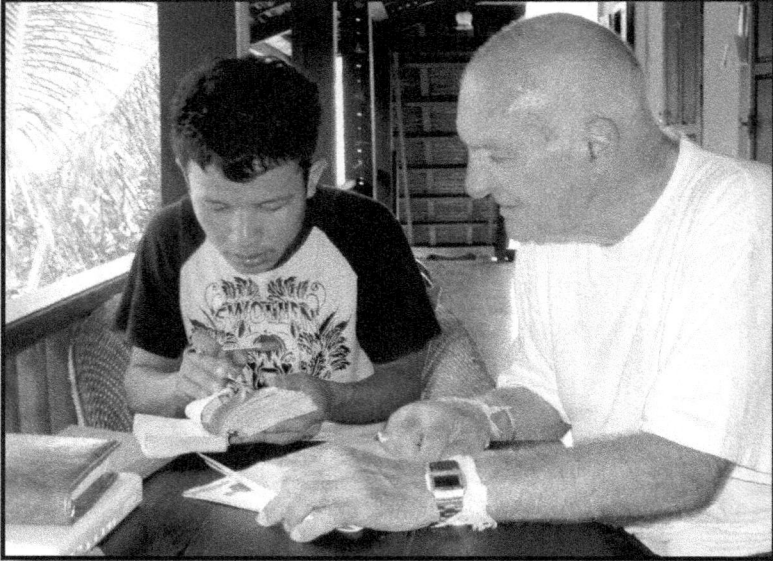

Starting English lessons with Chanthy

We sit in the garden of Khoumxiengthong and also on our verndah and from the very start we have fun. Chanthy is initially shy but also quick and keen to learn. First Iain reads aloud the small stories from the books to give them the correct flow and pronunciation. Chanthy then reads the same story aloud a couple of times, with us correcting his pronunciation, especially encouraging him to complete the end of words. After that he has a go at the comprehension and grammar questions, filling in the blanks in pencil. Simple stuff. But that's it isn't it? The simple stuff is the best and at a level with which we all feel comfortable. Person to person. Face to face. Lots of laughs. Mind you there were a few surprises too. The first came fairly early on.

Iain: *Do you know what this is?* (picking up the key ring from which dangled the key to the motorbike that Chanthy often borrows from one of his myriad cousins. It also has a miniature Eiffel Tower hanging from it.)

Chanthy: *A stupa.*

Iain: (slightly taken aback) *Well, yes, it is a stupa (a Buddhist shrine) in a sort of a way of I guess, but no. It's a big tower called the Eiffel Tower and its in Paris. Do you know where Paris is?*

Chanthy: *London.*

Iain: *Not quite. Paris is the capital of France. London is the capital of England. Hold on a mo and I'll show you a map.*

For just such occasions we always travel with a medium-sized world map. We spread it out and give a bit of a geography lesson, pointing out Laos, Luang Prabang and Vientiane, the surrounding countries of Vietnam, Cambodia, Thailand, Myanmar and China, then Paris and London and of course Australia and Sydney, 'where our son and his family live', we explain, because its the one Australian city most people know about. Finally we reach the United States, New York, San Francisco, 'where our daughter lives' and Washington, the capital.

Chanthy regards the map quietly for a few moments before asking, 'Where is the ocean?'

Iain: (after a slight pause) *Okay. Well you see all*

this green and brown; those are the continents, the land, and the mountains. But all the blue and as you can see, there's much more blue, that's all the oceans: the Pacific, the Atlantic, the Indian Ocean and so on.

Chanthy: After studying the map more closely. *'There's a lot of ocean,'*

We agreed.

Chanthy: *Is it deep?* and seeing our look of puzzlement, *'The ocean, is it deep? As deep as the Mekong?'*

We assure him that yes the oceans are very deep; deeper, much deeper than the Mekong. Iain goes on to explain a bit about shifting tectonic plates, the deep ocean trenches and so forth, while Chanthy just nods pensively. His view of the world, having grown up in a land-locked country has just shifted perspective dramatically. In some ways we feel sorry about that.

Chanthy tells us stories of his day: how many, or few, customers Konkhai had, what they ordered, what they said, how they behaved. Doubtless most of these diners imagine only that they are in Laos having new experiences and meeting new people; whereas they are in fact educating Chanthy about the outside world. Everything about the way they ate, moved, dressed, spoke, it all registered with him. The stories he tells are never judgmental, that is not in his nature, but to a village boy they are a revelation.

Really it is something of the same for us at Khoumxiengthong. Guests come and go, most staying only a few days. In a short while we become adept at spotting the ones who are 'getting it' and those who might just as well have stayed home, viewed a travel documentary on Laos and sent the monies they had spent on getting to and being in Laos to an aid organization. The visitors come from all around the world.

Frequently, after noticing that we tuck ourselves away on the upstairs balcony, typing away at our computers, rather than rushing out to visit wats and museums, other visitors ask what we are up to and we become adept at giving a short spiel about e-publishing and how it can be done anywhere as long as you have access to the Internet.

The one 'event' we do leave our worktable for is the beating of the drum. This happens at 4pm, during two periods in each month, for two days each side of new moon and two days each side of full moon and lasts for ten minutes. It also occurs at 4am for the same duration during the same period of the moon.

Our big room, overlooking the back courtyard of the Sirimounkoun Sayaram Wat, is little more than twenty metres or so from that wat's big drum and acts as something of a reverb, so the deep sound is magnified and booms around the walls throbbing in our eardrums. We always planned to get up in the dark for the early morning happening, but we never do, in fact after several months of being jolted awake we even begin to enjoy the drumming and incorporate it into our sleep patterns.

When the drumming starts up in the afternoons we use it as a time signal that we should take a break from our computer screens. On occasions when Chanthy is not with us we desert our leafy aerie and make the short walk around into the courtyard of 'our' wat to enjoy the visual spectacle. This is how we pick up our second English language student.

We watch a handsome muscular young novice thwack away rhythmically and with enormous force at the large hanging drum, obviously getting great enjoyment as well as physical pleasure from his mastery of this skill. Below him stands a far slighter-built novice who keeps perfect timing on a pair of cymbals. Pure theatre. Small knots of other novices stand vigil in obvious appreciation of their talent. Visitors, attracted by the sounds, come to watch.

In the humidity and increasing heat of Spring, the drummer works up quite a sweat and when he completes the last phrasing, always with a flourish of abandonment, he jumps athletically down the small set of steps from the bell-tower rubbing the soreness from his hands, but with a smile of contentment over a job well done.

Khamchanh, as we came to know him, Khamchanh Bounprasird is his full name, soon realizes that we were not drop-by-briefly visitors and begins to make conversation with Iain, who expresses his delight in his drumming skills. I am conscious that it is customary for women to stand slightly apart and not to touch a monk or novice although Khamchanh is only too happy to talk to me as well as Iain

We quickly learn that Khamchanh, like Chanthy, is also eighteen, but that the two young men have experienced very different childhoods. Khamchanh had become a novice when he was only eleven. Since then he has lived at the wat, studying full time at the Monk's School not far from his wat, nearer the centre of town. He does go to his home village, a couple of hours away by bus, still in Luang Prabang Province, for infrequent short visits. His family, especially his Mum and Dad, also visit him on occasions. But essentially the wat is his home and the other dozen novices, his family.

As I've mentioned, there are around thirty wats in Luang Prabang, home, in this sense, to perhaps three thousand novices and a few score of fully initiated monks. Their orange robes are omnipresent. Their self-effacing mode of gliding, as distinct from walking, usually in pairs, along the streets throughout the day, mostly to and from classes, means they form the town's spiritual glue and a calm background to everybody's daily life.

Iain and I talk about how different the atmosphere of Luang Prabang would be if, instead of novices in orange robes, the streets were filled with three thousand young men wearing jeans and tee-shirts, hanging out together in groups, as similar-aged men in our home society do.

It is very evident, from our first conversation with him, that Khamchanh has far-ranging interests and is a compulsive thinker. Unsure of what was and what was not okay to bring into conversations, Iain begins by mentioning his own interest in space research and science. Khamchanh immediately latches on to this and so it is that an issue of *The Planetary Report*, a magazine Iain has subscribed to for decades and that had just arrived in a bundle of mail on-sent from home, is the first printed matter we share with Khamchanh.

He also immediately takes it as natural that we visit him daily and so we slip into the routine of walking around the wall at 8am to sit in the shade of the huge frangipani trees, for him to read aloud from books he has brought back from the library at the Monk's School and to discuss their contents.

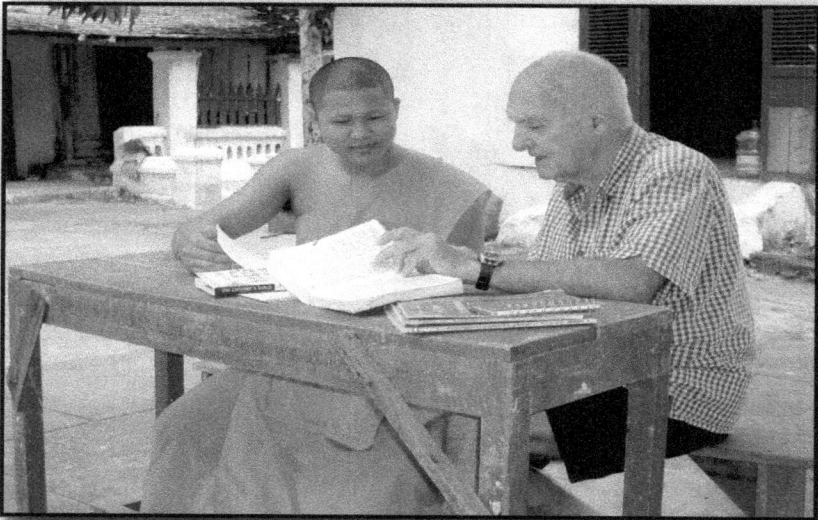

In the courtyard of Sirimounkoun Sayaram Wat with Khamchanh

It was a very eclectic mix from Buddhism, that he quickly sensed I was open to talking about, through geography and physics to soccer, modern history and yes, politics, though about this last area we are always extremely circumspect.

Laos, you have to keep reminding yourself, operates under a Communist Party system. Buddhism had been given the boot when the change of government occurred in 1975. Wats had been closed, novices returned to their villages and monks forced to work in the fields.

The Party had long realized, correctly of course, that the Buddhist Sangha, their Community or Association, which is somewhat comparable to an ad hoc mixture of the Church of England Synod and the Vatican Council of the Catholic Church, has entrenched real power and authority.

Those having so recently won political power would have taken note of what at that time were recent street demonstrations by monks and novices in Vietnam, during which there were self-immolations and the effect this had on the general population. They were not going to leave themselves open to the impact of behaviour like that. So they moved quickly and decisively against religious adherence.

But, just as with the banning of the nop, it didn't take long for the new government to realise and accept that shutting the wats and banning Buddhism wasn't a workable solution. Religious beliefs were, as they still are, too deeply entrenched in people's daily lives to be able to simply issue edicts to annul them.

After less than a year wats were allowed to become places of worship again, monks and novices took up residence and the centuries old practice of monks' schools was re-established. Which was just as well, because the appalling void of an education system left in the wake of over a hundred years of French colonial rule meant that for many children learning at a monk's school was their only educational opportunity.

The Communist Party of the Central Government and the Buddhist Sangha has hammered out some form of compromise that is unfathomable, at least to outsiders. In a very Buddhist way of dealing with the situation, all students at the monks' schools compulsorily attend classes in Lao politics.

'Have you ever heard of a man called Hitler?' Khamchanh asks in one of our 8am get-togethers when the quickly rising temperature and humidity had already drained the brain. We assure him we have.

'I saw a programme about him on Thai television last night.'

'Television?!' we groan.

Khamchanh gives his gentle smile. 'My abbot has one in his room and he sometimes invites me to watch it with him. What do you know about this Hitler.'

We are late to breakfast that morning and Khamchanh was late to class. But we all learnt a lot; Khamchanh about European history and us about another take on evil, a Buddhist perspective. We require two cups of coffee to gain our equilibrium. This teaching is also a learning.

It is shortly after this that Thiemchanh, our landlady and Noi's long-suffering wife, comes up to our verandah one afternoon with a plate of coconut sticky rice wrapped in banana leaves. She frequently presents us with small gifts of her delicious home-cooked food; spicy noodle soup, banana fritters, freshly opened coconuts. But on this day she comes with something additional under her arm, a number of notebooks. Diffidently she opens these to share with us and we are astounded to see page after page of small, careful, neat English script.

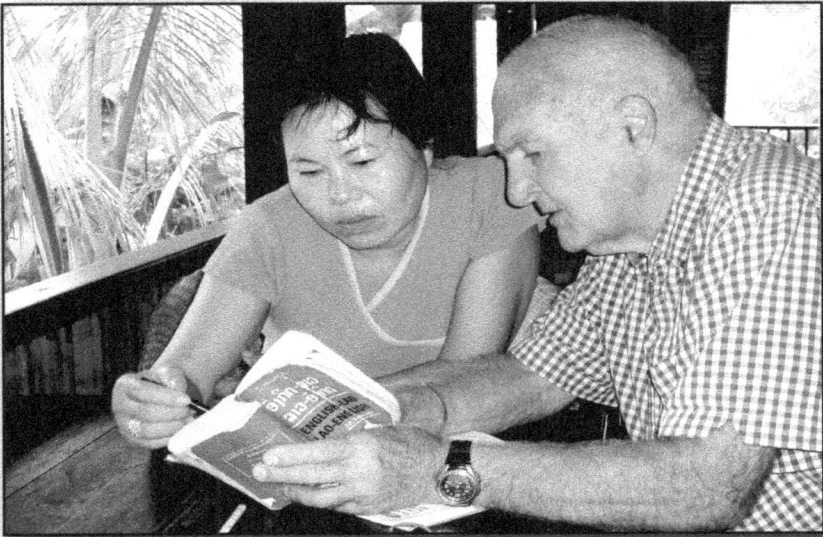

With our landlady, Thiemchanh

'Did you do all this?' we inquire. Thiemchanh nods and gives a small smile of embarrassment as we enthuse over her work. At this point we realize we have taken on our third student! e

Thiemchanh's back-story is totally different from that of our other two learners. For starters she is more than a couple of decades older than Chanthy and Khamchanh. She would have experienced first hand the initial huge social turmoil the change of government wrought. In Lao terms she is financially well-to-do. She is not a member of one of the thirteen, or is it seven, families; the stories vary, whom we are frequently told, run the country. But she has those all important social connections and she has property.

She also has her husband, Noi and three sons. The oldest, Chanthaek, who is 22, has finished university and is finding out what he might want to pursue as a career. For the present he is having a go in the hotel industry. At 19 Chanthaboun is at university and 16 year-old Chanthaphone is still in high school. In as far as it is possible in Laos, the family atmosphere at Khoumxiengthong feels testosterone driven. There are motorbikes, computer games, lounging young men and visiting girlfriends.

Noi, the friendly face of the guesthouse, is the meeter and greeter of potential clients. He chats on effusively in his own highly idiosyncratic version of English.

Behind all this, holding together the fabric of family life, is self-effacing Thiemchanh whom we now discover had sufficient education to have studied English for four years. All she needs from us is the encouragement of her self-confidence that had been all but obliterated in her all-male household.

We arrange that she will come up to our balcony desk for an hour starting at 7am, before the guests are served their simple breakfast. We do this seven days a week and begin by reading through the work she had done years before, when she was a single woman, after which we progress on to books from Carol Kresge's wide supply at *My Library*.

At first there are rather frequent interruptions by one or other of the males in Thiemchanh's life. Chanthaphone can't find a clean shirt for school. Chanthaboun wants to use his mother's motorbike to get to uni because his doesn't have enough petrol in his own and Chantha wants to tell his mother that his girlfriend will be picking him up from work. Even Noi comes to inquire of her where the pencils are that guests need to fill in their breakfast request forms.

Gradually, with encouragement from us, they all come to realize that the hour between 7am and 8am is Thiemchanh's time and that she is out of bounds for them and their domestic requests.

As those changes occur so too do modifications in Thiemchanh's personality. She becomes more self-confident, courageous even and it is a great joy to be involved in her growth.

So our life is transformed and enriched. From 7am to 8am we encourage wife and mother

Thiemchanh and watch her blossom as an independent woman. We then walk around the low wall dividing the garden of Khoumxiengthong from Wat Sirimounkhoun and share challenging ideas with novice Khamchanh. After that we breakfast often at Le Banneton, the French café opposite the wat. Then we settle down to a day's work, trying to establish our e-publishing business, so that by 4.00 pm we are ready for the welcome break provided by the appearance of the always positively cheerful Chanthy, with stories about his customers or news of what is happening in his village of NaLin.

I have gone into all this detail because so many people ask: 'How did you meet these people?' or 'How did you start doing this?' The more up front ones also ask, 'How could you afford to do it?'

So I'll answer that too, in order to dispel the always present, though unspoken inference that we could do it because we could somehow more easily afford to. That is untrue. We did what a large number of people who ask those questions could also do; we rented out our family home. The moderate rent we received covered the cost of our room at Khoumxiengthong and our meals. Nothing clever, fancy or high moral ground; just a matter of wanting to do something badly enough that you re-allocate your resources and take a leap into the unknown.

5

FIRST BASI

It was amidst all of this that we felt strongly motivated to suggest to Chanthy that we would like to pay his school fees for the next school year.

We were coming to the end of one of our daily English language sessions that we usually finished by having a general chat. Chanthy's grasp of grammar, sentence construction and general syntax had come on by leaps and bounds. Even his pronunciation had showed marked improvement, though I did get tired of hearing myself repeat a word he had used and asking him to say it again but this time adding the final letter. So that 'how' became house, 'plea' became please and 'enou' became enough.

What had also helped with all of this was his growth in personal confidence. Often he came with a list of words he had heard used by clients at

45

Konkhai restaurant or spoken on the Thai television programmes beamed in to Laos. These are naturally more popular than the local TV productions that often consist for the main part of endless screenings of Party Meetings attended by men in awful suits or in even more awful military uniforms.

Despite their inbuilt reservations about their neighbours, both the Lao and Thai of course have rather a lot in common, including similarities in language that make it possible for them to easily understand each other, even when speaking their own individual tongue.

Thai television presents a very different world from that in which most Lao people live. So close, yet so far, but even so, it is difficult to pick up any sense of envy on the part of the Lao for these far more affluent neighbours.

Just to look across the river from Vientiane, even though that river is the mighty Mekong and to view so easily the Thai streetlights and houses; to know through intimate contact, that over there exists perhaps employment, as well as far better social infrastructure, in the way of schools, hospitals and comparatively decent housing, would surely be a challenge.

On this particular day Chanthy didn't talk about the latest Thai television soap opera. These always contained liberal doses of ghosts and spirits that so genuinely terrified him he had to hold his hands over his eyes and often had nightmares in which the bodies of the bloodied dead appeared. We had tried unsuccessfully to josh him out of these fears but though he took our jokes in good humour, he was unconvinced. Lao people generally are heavily into the spirit world.

Instead, today we talk more about his village childhood. He explains how after finishing primary school in the riverside village of Hadsaikham, a daily walk of an hour each way from his home, he had continued his education at the District Centre of Muang Nam. This was the closest place where there was a secondary school.

Iain: *How far away was that?*

Chanthy: *Three or four hours.*

Trish: *You did that every day!*

Chanthy: *No. I walked there on Sunday night and stayed with a friend of my father for the week. Then I walked home on Friday to help my parents on their farm.*

Iain: *How old were you then?*

Chanthy: *Since I was ten.*

Iain: *And you did that for all your years at high school?*

Chanthy: (nodding) *Sometimes the road is too bad, the mud so deep I have to go another way. But that is over three mountains so it is quite hard.*

The three of us are sitting on the verandah shaded by big palm trees and breathing in the perfume of frangipani and jasmine. Iain and I are conjuring up in our mind's eye the image of a young boy who was so determined to get an education because he knew it was the first step in the hard-scrabble climb out of poverty.

What about when it rained? Iain asks.

Chanthy looks momentarily puzzled by so strange a question. Then with a big smile, he says,

I carry an umbrella.

Well of course, Iain says and we all laugh.

That night in bed we several times repeat those questions and answers between ourselves. Freighted as they were with so much matter-of-factness and we always finished up with the umbrella response.

'I am glad,' Iain says softly into the dark of the moon free night, 'we offered to pay his college fees. He deserves a break.'

Chanthy had accepted our offer with that same grace we had witnessed previously and that had made for such ease between us. No embarrassment. No awkward words to make us feel we were being bountiful. Just a quiet thank you.

But the offer quickly led to a further, unanticipated, experience when a week or so later Chanthy arrived for his daily session beaming with pleasure at the news he had to impart.

'My mother and father, when I told them Dear Trish Dear Iain will pay for my study, they say we must have a basi.'

Honorifics, such as Mr. Mrs. or Ms. play a very important descriptive role in social interactions in Laos. Used as a form of address, everyone is thereby made aware of where that person stands in relation to everyone else. Unable to find a title that fitted our relationship, after all we were not his Mother, Father, Grandparents, Uncle, Aunt or even the broad generic Cousin, Chanthy now began always to refer to us in speech and in writing as *Dear*.

But what was a basi? When I did a bit of research in Robert Cooper's excellent guide, *The Lao, Laos ...and you* I found he describes it as a 'soul support ceremony.' So okay, whose soul can't do with a bit of support.

The Lao soul, it would appear comes in thirty-two khwan or pieces. Expressed in simplistic lay language these khwan have the disturbing habit of wandering off, becoming lost or at least displaced and for a person, or at least their soul, to become entire or whole again, these bits and pieces need to be called home and reunited into one whole. A sort of 'Come in number forty-nine, your time is up,' idea and not a bad one at that.

This is more an animist concept than Buddhist. It seems to belong to the same spheres of thought as the *phii*, the spirits; the ones for whom we were to see Noi leaving out little balls of sticky rice on New

Year's Eve. Something along the lines of placing bowls of milk with some cookies by the Christmas tree to fortify Santa and his helpers on Christmas Eve. I find these similarities a very consoling sign of common humanity.

Chanthy is extremely excited about the prospect of the basi. It was to be held on a Saturday at his Uncle's house in Luang Prabang which is where he lived, or at least slept, on a thin, rolled up mattress. He told us, his eyes glittering with emotion, that both his parents were coming up from his village to meet us and his older brother was taking time off from his job on the buses in order to be there. We began to realise and accept the importance of the occasion.

'This is the first basi for me since I was a baby,' he says with a huge happy grin.

Chanthy's Uncle lives in Phosi village on the outskirts of Luang Prabang. When he picks us up in a cousin's tuk-tuk to make the fifteen-minute journey across town, he honestly looked as though he might literally burst through his skin with excitement and his English had all but deserted him.

The extremely simple, two storey, small brick, tin-roofed house, squeezed in at the end of a rutted lane was abuzz with activity when the tuk-tuk driver/cousin dropped us off among a flurry of gawping village children.

We are introduced to Chanthy's mother, Buachanh, his father, Thongkhan, both of them small of stature, sinewy and brown-skinned from working in their rice paddy. His brother Jai, older than Chanthy by two years, comes forward: stiff and ill at ease. We also meet Aunt Thongmee, his grandfather's sister, more rounded and with relaxed warm gestures. After that it is a blur of names and faces and I never did work out to which of the many uncles present this house belonged.

In the tiny space we feel proportionally large-bodied, gawky and sweaty. It was difficult not to take up too much space.

Without any preliminary social niceties, explanations or chitchat the ceremony starts. All we could do was watch what others did and follow their lead.

We are both given a scarf and instructed in how to drape this across the left shoulder so as to cover the heart. What I later learnt is called a *phakhoum*, an offering to the spirit world, is then placed in the middle of the room and everyone else kneels back on their ankles on the thin cloth covering the hard floor. The best our stiff-jointed western legs and bottoms accustomed to soft sofas could manage, is a sideways squat.

Shaped like a miniature Christmas tree, the *phakhoum* is built up from layers of marigold blossoms interspersed with pungently perfumed white flower heads. The flower-tree grows in diminishing layers til it finishes in a cone of palm

51

leaf from which protrudes a series of marigold encrusted wooden skewers. Nestled among these, at the very peak, is a candle that is now being lit.

The flower-tree rests in a large metal bowl decorated with an elaborately beaten design and this in turn sits on a big metal tray. The tray is laden with sugar bananas, small oranges, rice cakes, packets of dried fruits, a small tumbler full of what smells like mineral turpentine but is in fact the firewater liquor lao-lao, plus a dead, cooked chook, its plucked body twisted and trussed so it's beak is unnaturally close to its anus.

At the base of the *phakhoum* itself there are more wooden skewers from which hang cut pieces of unbleached cotton. All this is the handiwork of Aunt Thongmee who nods her head in appreciation as we admire her piece of art.

But there is no time for enlarging upon our praise because with no introduction or formalities an elderly man sitting cross-legged beside me begins to chant in piercingly high-tone Pali. The calling in of the spirit pieces is underway.

At this point an inner circle of people including, with stifled groans, Iain and I, comes forward on their knees and we all place our fingertips on the *phakhoum*-bearing tray. From the circle of bodies behind us people reach forward and touch the shoulders of those in front. We are joined as one and even someone as sceptical and faith-free as myself could not fail to experience the vibration that runs from body to body. The hair stands up on the back of my neck. My mind seems to leave my body. There is a micro-instant of simultaneously indrawn breath. There is Something. Then, just as suddenly as it had come it is gone. Over. Done.

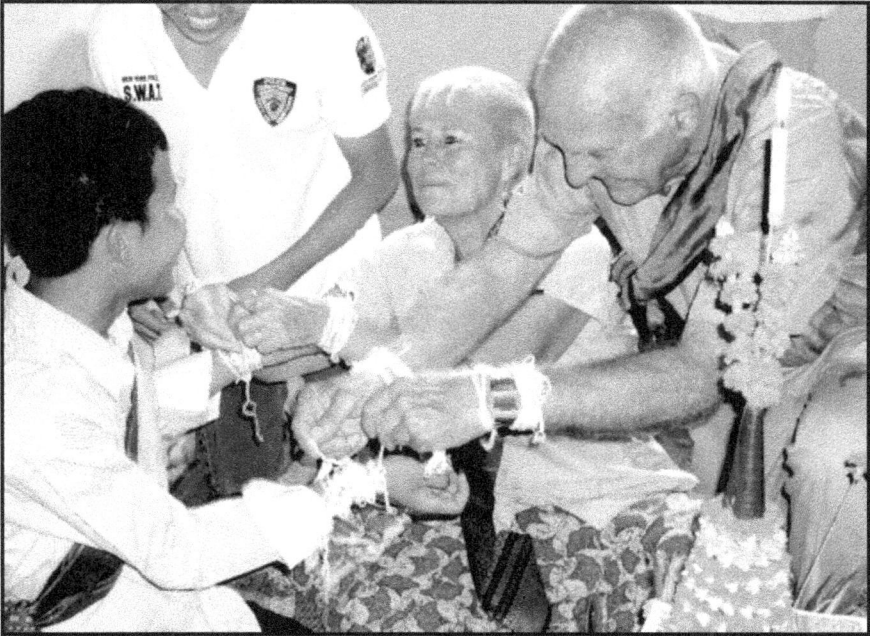

Tying *phii su kwan* spirit strings around each others' wrists

The spell broken, everyone talks at once, seeming both released and relieved while we immediately became the centre of attraction. Our wrists are gently grasped and the strands of cut cotton, the *Phii Su Kwan* spirit strings, taken from the *phakhoun* are tied around them. Chanthy signals that we should hold our other hand up to our bowed forehead in a sort of one-handed nop, but this is impossible because both wrists are grasped, as are his too. As the strings are tied, words that are good wishes, are whispered and our flesh pressed. The heat, magnified by the tin

roof, makes us both sweat embarrassingly profusely. Aunt Thongmee kneels at my side fanning my reddened face all the while smiling encouragement. I later find out that she was born in the same year as me. Sisterhood.

Lao-lao is drunk, but only after small drops of it are flicked skywards, for the gods. Sticky rice and vegetables are eaten. Chanthy must have forewarned them about our strange non-meat-eating habits. Flesh is torn from the chicken and distributed to the others. There is a huge sense of community, of togetherness and belonging.

Chanthy, partly obscured, with parents
Buachanh and Thongkhan

The cousin returns in his tuk-tuk and Chanthy insists on seeing us back to our guesthouse. All the way he talks, or rather gabbles, about the experience. It takes him several days to come back down to mere earth!

6

PI MAI

The days blur into weeks and then months. The humid heat intensifies from staggering to outrageous and everyone begins muttering the words Pi Mai, Pi Mai, Pi Mai, like an incantation for longed for relief.

Pi Mai is the celebration of Lao New Year. The energy around the weeklong festival is like Christmas, New Year, a 21st, a wedding and Sydney's Mardi Gras all rolled together and topped with a touch of Grand Final fever; but with a blessedly minimal commercial overlay. We are about to celebrate the beginning of the year 2553 in the Buddhist calendar and the entire town emanates anticipation.

The perimeter walls of our wat and all the others in the main street, are given a coat of whitewash, slopped on with carefree abandon by the novices. These same young men carefully touch up the

56

complex gold, black and red designs on the exteriors of wat buildings.

The lion figures guarding the wide steps down to the Mekong are whitewashed and their gaping mouths, plus the tips of their outsized penises are given a casual splashing of brilliant red.

The sinuous shapes of the mythological seven-headed naga that flows alongside each side of the entrance to one of the main wats are made even more threatening by receiving a dramatic coating of silver paint while the inside of their gaping jaws, that spew forth seven more no less terrifying nagas, are also daubed with scarlet.

The seven-headed Naga

A hum of continuous chanting in Pali, the ancient Indian script and the liturgical language of Theravada Buddhism, rises from the wats.

'Elephants', an excited Noi calls up to us one early morning and we gallop down the stairs to see three of the great, grey animals lumber past in the laneway outside our house, their huge bodies painted with brightly coloured designs. Thiemchanh gives us small bananas and we pluck up the nerve to offer them out on the flat of our palms.

Every wat becomes a mass of flowers and each day we see families, dressed in their best, bringing along yet more. They often stay to listen to a dhet, a dharma talk, given by the wat's abbot, who sits cross-legged on a mat in one of the outer buildings. Daily there are ceremonies in which Buddha figures are bathed with lustral water.

In a typical Lao mix of the spiritual with the more corporeal, in the courtyard of Wat Xiengthong novices sell tiny scrolls of paper for very small amounts of kip. These are chosen at random by the novices from wooden boxes divided into many partitions and carry messages, in Pali script that no one other than monks and novices can understand nowadays. These are read aloud to the anxious listeners who, judging by their expressions, are all relieved with the telling of good news. Fortune telling.

Street stalls appear, selling brightly coloured, garishly patterned, cheap, cotton shirts imported from Thailand.

Half the rooms in our guesthouse are taken over by Noi and Thiemchanh's visiting family and friends ranging in age from four through to elderly. Mattresses and clothes are scattered and strewn all over the place and lots of giggling can be heard coming from rooms; a bit like Christmas at our place!

The date of the major street procession is announced, though as always it is impossible to pin down an exact time. On a stupendously hot night we cycle along to a packed open sports ground at the edge of town to witness the choosing of Miss Pi Mai.

Bright neon lights, the smell of cooking, stalls selling kitsch knick-knacks, wide-eyed children and scrounging dogs. Over it all a cacophony of loud, distorted music. It is a delight.

Up on stage the row of contestants all look identical, any differences blurred to insignificance by pore-clogging quantities of make up and identical hairstyles. Ms. Er in her wedding outfit would fit right in. Gold and red are the colours of choice for the body-hugging sinhs and tops.

Glad-handing the microphone is a man who has the patter and the moves of someone who has obviously done it all, dozens of times, before. A couple of politicians, always such stand-outs, with their dyed comb-overs and shocking suits, speak a few words; no doubt the same few words all politicians all around the world spout forth at such events. It doesn't matter that these words are drowned by feedback because no one listens to them. They are too busy eating large fried insects, washed down with hot soft drinks from refilled bottles. Everyone is having a splendid time.

At dawn the following morning, we are still feeling a little seedy from the previous night's events when Noi presents us with an elaborate palm leaf and marigold flower confabulation, nopping like mad and saying 'Sabaidee Pi Mai Lao' over and over. After that he proceeds to place small balls of sticky rice in various niches and crannies around the house and garden, 'to feed the *phii*, spirits', he says. Having a bob or two each way I think you'd call that. Next he informs us, 'Phabang coming' and because by this time I am quick at picking up his gesticulated clues, I understand that if we are to experience this event we should change from our shorts and tee-shirts into something more *napteu* which I now know means respect. Fair enough.

The Phabang is the Lao Holy of Holies: the embodiment of the national spirit. It is after this statue that the spiritual capital of Laos, Luang Prabang is named. Except for the period of Pi Mai this Khymer-style standing Buddha, made from an alloy of gold, silver and bronze and only a little under a metre tall, is kept on view in a small barred room at the side of the Royal Palace Museum. On every one of our several visits to the Museum there was always a sizeable number of visitors making full obeisance in front of these bars.

For the Lao there are a myriad stories attached to this sacred statue. The most prevalent is that the Thais stole the original statue in the late 1700s and again in the early 1800s. In Lao stories the Thais are always the bad guys, whether historically or in the present. When it was eventually returned in 1867, it is said that the cunning, conniving Thais had replaced it with a copy. It is also reported that the original is in Moscow. Perhaps 'borrowed' by the Russians during their time in Laos during the chaotic sixties and seventies when everyone was in for what they could get out.

Original or copy, what we are keen to see is the ceremony surrounding the Phabang's perambulation from the Royal Palace along the main street to Wat Mai Suwannaphumaham where it will reside, scrupulously watched over by a rotational bevy of monks, for the climactic four days of Pi Mai.

We are certainly glad we have changed our clothes for the occasion. Not that we could in any way come up to the standard of the finery of Luang Prabang's top set. Men and women are turned out in immaculately presented silken finery of nineteenth century styling: the men's the more impressive by being topped with a spiffo style of turban. If appearances are anything to go by then these are Royalists to a man and woman.

To the accompaniment of loud drums, tinny bugles and clashing cymbals the Phabang, wrapped in a golden cloak is placed, with great veneration, on the symbolic sedan chair of power and hung over and about with more golden cloths. All this is then raised, gently and carefully, by way of carrying poles slung across the shoulders of an eight-some of men dressed in bright coloured satin and silk pantaloons and shirts, topped by out of place Jester caps.

The Phabang is carried from the Royal Palace to Wat Mai Suwannaphumaham

The dense crowd of worshippers lining the circular pathway through the Palace grounds falls totally silent. They kneel, bow and nop as one. There is no doubting the depth of their emotion.

The Phabang is carried, followed by a large crowd, in reverent quietude a little distance along the main street and into the precinct of Wat Mai.

As we follow the procession out onto the main road we meet Noi and Thiemchanh's three sons coming down from their dawn climb up the steep steps of Phousi Hill where they have been to welcome in the New Year.

Later, in the literally stunning heat, the family, the youngest of whom, 16-year-old Chanthaphone, we barely recognise, again summons us into the street. Chanthaphone's entire body has been painted black; he is wearing a very Ghandi-like dhoti and is pretending to stagger about with the aid of a walking stick. He is the somewhat spoiled joker of the family. By contrast Noi is apparelled in his very best smart gear and carries armfuls of tropical blossoms collected from their garden.

A blackened Chantaphone ready for the parade

The parade is coming, they say, assuring us this is the best spot from which to enjoy it. 'But be careful of your camera,' they warn before they all stride off down the street to mingle with the on-rush of the parade we can now hear approaching.

Some parade! For more than an hour it streams past us and around the corner along to Wat Xiengthong. Teams of young girls in vivid coloured costumes and equally vivid makeup, young boys in purple silk trousers wearing grim masks to terrorise small children, men dressed as roaring lions and troupes of men dressed as hissing snakes. Groups of diverse minority people such as Khmu and Hmong in their traditional hand-stitched clothing and of course, assorted eccentrics taking advantage of the anything-goes atmosphere, though no one other than Chanthaphone has painted their entire body black.

Part of the hour-long Pi Mai parade

Crowds line either side of the street, armed with small and not so small, buckets of water they refill from hoses or from kerbside open metal drums brimming with water. No one is sacrosanct not even the scores of orange-robed monks and novices. These sit impassively on moving floats in a lotus position, their hands resting in their laps and are drenched by the more daring young men who leap from the pavement and swill buckets full of water over their newly shaven heads. They never wipe their faces. They never grimace or turn away. They never smile. With their internal stillness they could be statues. The throwing of water is said to be symbolic of the washing out of the old year and a cleansing in preparation for the new. We understand now Noi's warning about our cameras.

Novices are also drenched with water during Pi Mai

There are other floats, drawn by sweating young blokes. Some of these carry posters with social messages that are pretty easy to decipher such as 'Say No to Drugs'. Some carry local dignitaries and politicians who do queen-like waves.

But the one everyone is waiting for and you can hear the roars of appreciation as it approaches, is the float of the mermaid and something that perhaps most resembles a unicorn on whose back reclines Miss Pi Mai. Fortunately for her she is protected from the blazing sun and too heavy a drenching by a huge painted parasol.

Miss Pi Mai

Iain manages to take some shots but it is at high risk to the camera, as we both receive a number of good-natured full-body slosh-overs.

The following day celebrations continue but this time the happening place to be is Hat Muang Khoum, an island in the middle of the Mekong River, reached by small, darting, river craft overcrowded with highly excited and in many cases inebriated people.

We wade up the sandy slope onto what is not much more than an extremely large sand bar and join in the building of elaborate sand stupas finally helping to decorate them with pennants displaying the mythical creatures of the Buddhist zodiac. Again there are stalls selling sizzling buffalo blood sausages and deep fried crickets as well as bottles of beer that are stored under huge blocks of rapidly melting ice.

We are not normally party people, so these days replete with happenings have taken their physical toll! The finishing touch is the return walk back to our room that evening. The street is crammed with so many people determined to squeeze the last little bit of juice out of the festivities that what is normally a casual twenty minute stroll turns into an hour-long squeeze through a press of hot flesh. In the midst of it all, the noise, the smell, the heat, a small stage had been erected and in the glare from arc lights a number of lavishly dressed lady-boys strut their stuff. Sequins, tassels, head-dresses, extra-high heels, extra-short skirts, feather boas, blonde wigs, over-sized costume jewellery and carefully contrived make-up. Despite, or perhaps because of the disguises, we readily spot a waiter from a restaurant we patronise regularly. We wave. S/he waved back and flashes a big happy smile.

That night a huge storm hits Luang Prabang and for hour after hour the lightening and thunder trapped by the surrounding mountains flashes and growls, accompanied by wind-powered goblets of drenching rain, so dense and large they crash on the rooves making sleep impossible until the early hours.

When we finally surface, after an exhausted sleep-in, we find the tall palm tree that had graced the next-door compound's main lawn has been torn whole from the ground and has speared into the dense wall of heavy foliage that separates our gardens.

We take our bicycles for a spin along the Mekong waterfront where big branches and whole trees lie strewn among the sheet metal fences that had surrounded the large building site on what had once been part of the Royal Palace. Minced leaves and shredded palm fronds carpet the road.

The island of Hat Muang Khoum has totally disappeared under the now raging waters of the Mekong. No trace can be seen of the sandcastles or beer and food stalls. The residents are all out on the streets beginning the massive job of cleaning up. But they smile and called Sabaidee to us, appearing content that this is a brand new year.

7

THE OTHER LIFE

It was shortly after this totally full-on weeklong experience that what we have come to think of as our 'other life' now starts to intrude at a pace.

Photographs arrive by email of our grand children that clearly show they are not the people they were when we last saw them. Our daughter, Zara emails from San Francisco to say she is coming with her boyfriend Jay Herda, whom we have not met, to visit us in Laos within a few weeks.

During our time in Luang Prabang, we have been beavering away on our verandah where we, well really it is mostly Iain, but together we have managed to get four of our books up on Amazon as e-publications and two available on Kindle electronic readers. We feel we have broken the ice and started on a new, late-life career-change!

The lease on our house will soon be up for renewal. We need to let our tenant know our plans.

There is an email from a photographer friend, Claire Leimbach, saying she will be in Mongolia for the annual Nadaam Festival in mid July and will we join her? Why not, we think.

But to get to meet up with Claire and to do some rough travel on our own in Mongolia requires time. It is not a country to rush through. So we begin to make plans. There is no Mongolian Embassy in Laos. Best, we decide, to get visas in Beijing which is also where we could get a train to travel across the Gobi Desert to the Mongolian capital of Ulaan Baatar.

A more interesting and appealing route to Beijing would be overland through northern Laos to Oudomxai, crossing the border at Boten and on into the southern Chinese Provinces of mountainous Yuannan and Schezhuan. Visas for China can be applied for in Vientiane.

The Annamite Range on the way to Vientiane

We take the eight-hour, that turns into ten-hour, bus trip down to the capital, journeying alongside the fantastical Lord-of-the Rings-like peaks of the Annamite Range that form a rugged and impressive barrier between Laos and Viet Nam.

It is only going to be a three-day trip away from Luang Prabang, but Chanthy insists on seeing us off from the bus station. His brother Jai, who you'll recall is working on the buses is not on our run to the capital that day. But having heard from Chanthy descriptions of how Jai, who is not a driver but a general dogsbody on the buses, sleeps in the luggage storage compartment and performs his ablutions in the bus station restrooms, we make sure to check out these 'facilities.' Not good. Little wonder Jai had appeared somewhat disconsolate at the basi ceremony where we met him.

Zara and Jay arrive shortly after our return to Luang Prabang. Zara has always been an excellent travel companion, easy, adaptable, up for anything and able to get along with anyone because she is genuinely interested in everyone. So we hold no fears about her ability to adapt to a bit of time in south east Asia from her relatively comfortable life in San Francisco.

Unknown Jay comes up trumps too and we enjoy taking time away from our computers to play tourist with them.

We go by riverboat up the Mekong to see again the hundreds of Buddha images crammed into the caves at Pak Ou. We take a tuk-tuk out for a swim at

Kuang Si waterfalls. By bicycle we visit the wats, the Royal Palace Museum, the Traditional Arts and Ethnology Centre and the confronting UXO, Unexploded Ordnance Centre. We attend a performance of the Royal Ballet Theatre and take Lao cooking lessons. We have massages, eat at restaurants and cafés and wander through the wonderful Night Market.

We introduce them to some of the people we have come to know, including Thiemchanh, our landlady and her family. Noi had welcomed them by leaving bunches of flowers on their bed. Also to our novice friend Khamchanh who, always wanting to learn more, queries them about their lives in San Francisco.

Then of course to Chanthy, to whom Zara gives a pile of storybooks for the children of his home village of NaLin purchased at *Big Brother Mouse*. Operating on a not-for profit-basis, this is a small Lao-owned and operated publishing business with a big heart whose slogan is 'Books that make literacy fun.' Anyone wanting to make a positive long-term impact in Laos should look them up on Google.

Mid-way through their visit we stay overnight at a riverside elephant camp not far from Luang Prabang where the unforgettable highlight of the entire trip for Zara comes as she and of course Jay and the two of us, swim with and wash and help to scrub down half a dozen huge elephants.

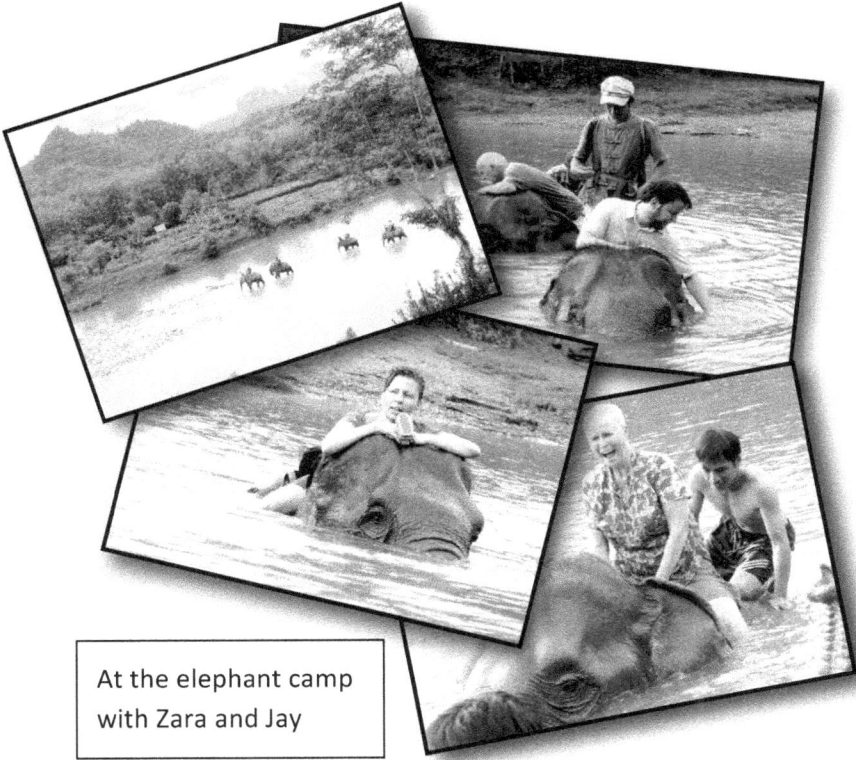

At the elephant camp
with Zara and Jay

Struggling to release its human population from the grip of poverty, Laos must, in addition, face up to its international responsibility of being home to the most of the world's severely dwindling numbers of Asian elephants. Camps such as the one we all stayed at help raise to consciousness of both visitors and locals about the reasons why it is vitally important that these great animals are enabled and encouraged to survive and thrive.

The unforgettable moment for Chanthy happens as Zara and Jay are leaving when Zara asks him, 'May I give you a hug?' Chanthy nods, unsure what to expect and what to do. He stands mute; his arms limp at his sides as she envelops him in a warm embrace. In a small voice he says 'Oh, thank you.'

Then and it seemed to happen so quickly, we too are leaving, though my heart was asking, 'why are we going?' So it was a happy relief when a few days before our planned leaving date Chanthy issued an invitation.

'When you come back from Mongolia, my Mother and Father would like you to visit them in their village of NaLin'. We gladly accept. Blissfully unaware of how this would change our lives.

Chanthy knows only a little less about Mongolia than we do at this time. He certainly has no idea about why we feel compelled to go there. But in another of those displays of open reception that we find so attractive in Lao thinking, he simply accepts our decision and again comes to wave us off on a bus, this time travelling north.

8

FIRST VISIT TO NALIN

By now you, the reader, are probably saying to yourself, its chapter eight already. When is she going to get to The Road this book is supposed to be about? Now they're heading off to China and Mongolia!

Yes, you are right. It is about time we found out about The Road. Though I hope the previous chapters have proved somewhat useful as a simple primer on Laos and the Lao and how and why we became involved.

In any event, by late 2011, after completing some twelve and a half thousand kilometres of overland journeying by train, buses and mini-buses, cars and trucks, we are back in Luang Prabang, being welcomed by Noi and Thiemchanh to our same accommodation at Khoumxiengthong, settling into more 'teaching' and with Chanthy making plans for our visit to his home village of NaLin.

NaLin is a three-hour boat trip down the Mekong, an adventure in itself, elevated to a great intensity by the fact that just now the floodwaters are at their height: swirling and eddying around barely concealed rocks, so the skipper really has to know what he is about.

Buying fruit & veg for the visit to NaLIn

Boarding the boat for the 3-hour trip down the Mekong at the start of the visit to NaLin

We are in a 30-plus-metre boat; a metal hull with a timber superstructure, locally built and owned by one of Chanthy's many, many uncles, or perhaps a cousin, of which there are even more!

We've already been to the early morning market and stocked up on buffalo meat, live fish, tropical veggies and fruit plus herbs and spices; everything that will be needed to feed the crowd who Chanthy tells us is coming to the basi welcoming ceremony

The journey has been a source of much anticipation and some excitement, not only for us but also most especially for Chanthy who is so obviously looking forward to showing us his home village.

Earlier in the week we track it down on Google Earth. Chanthy's expression when we zoom down onto the 50 or so simple wooden dwellings that make up NaLin is one of total amazement. He can hardly speak. But once he recovers, he points out his home as well as his Mum and Dad's rice paddy.

The river trip is not the only way to get to NaLin. There is a main unsealed road which runs from Luang Prabang to the district centre township at Muang Nan, mentioned earlier on our return trip from the Elephant Festival. From here there is a further fifteen kilometers over a very basic dirt road and eventually a track, to reach the village of NaLin, or Ban NaLin, as it is called in Lao. The trip takes about three hours to cover the seventy kilometers to Muang Nan, and then, in the wet season, as it is at the time of our visit, a further hour or more to NaLin

The comparatively easiest way to get to NaLin, at this time of year, Chanthy assures us, is from Hadsaikham, another village on the Mekong from which it is about five kilometers to NaLin village; have a look at the map. So this is where we moor and clamber up the muddy bank to be greeted by polite stares from the inhabitants.

Chanthy had attended primary school in Hadsaikham so while we are waiting for his Dad to arrive to pick us up in a tok-tok, we go off through the village to check out his old school, a dilapidated mud-floored, tin-roofed, shambolic building, which is where the slow burn of anger, about both the French and the present government, begins to ignite. God Bless the French, but let them not be forgiven for what they did *not* leave behind; in the way of schools, hospitals, roads and general infrastructure, in return for the large colonial revenues made from coffee and rubber. Not to forget also that the current regime has been in power for 35 years, so there is surely more they could have done too.

The onomatopoeic sound of a tok-tok, a two-wheeled tractor, draws us back to the village, where Chanthy's Dad, Thongkhan, has arrived and where we load up the ice-box, borrowed for the occasion from the boat plus all the groceries etcetera for a journey of five kilometres, that should take no more than about fifteen minutes, but ends up taking us almost an hour.

I should perhaps explain here the difference between a '*tuk-tuk*', and a '*tok-tok*'. A tuk-tuk is a small, three-wheeled mini taxi, used in cities and towns through-out Laos. It has two small benches in the back on which about six passengers can sit facing each other while the driver sits on a motorcycle, built into the front of the vehicle, open to the weather, apart from a wind-shield and a tin roof.

A tok-tok is a much larger vehicle lengthwise and is entirely open to the elements. It is really a three-wheeled tractor, used throughout much of south east Asia for hauling produce, as well as passengers, around in the countryside. Its distinctive feature is the powerful little, slow-revving motor that sits atop the two front wheels. So it is really a four-wheeled vehicle, but the front wheels are so close together, it looks like a three-wheeler. Its all controlled by an operator/driver struggling with two-meter-long handles, like extended motorcycle handlebars, while sitting on an open wooden bench.

Bogged during our first visit to NaLin

The trip to NaLin village is something to be remembered! And as things turn out, something we couldn't forget. The rutted quagmire of a track is even harder on the rear end, mine! and the spine, than travel in Mongolia. The driver of the tok-tok uses all his strength and brute force to keep the machine going forward using three gears: two forward and one reverse. A couple of times it bucks him right off into the deep mud. Several times everyone gets off and pushes and heaves and shoves to get us through the boggiest stretches. It is extremely hot and humid, but there is plenty of good-natured banter.

We ford a stream and finally make it into the tiny hamlet.

NaLin

Chanthy is seriously excited! His Mum, Buachanh, welcomes us to their home; a timber house with the underneath bricked in and with a cement floor used as a storage area and living space. All the food is unloaded and a lunch of papaya salad and small river fish promptly prepared and served.

After the meal, eaten with the fingers while sitting on the floor and watched over with goggle-eyed interest from the doorway by a large number of small awe-stuck, but silent children, the rain comes; torrents of it in solid and tropically thick chunks, so everyone falls into a stuporous daze. Well Iain and I do anyway!

When it eases, rubber boots are borrowed and we are taken by Chanthy on a tour of his village,

The house where Chanthy was born and the remains of his primary school.. Both now demolished.

seeing the derelict wooden shack where he and his older brother and younger sister had been born; also the ramshackle remains of the primary school he attended. There is no clinic, no midwife and of course no doctor. The nearest medical assistance at the time, a one-hour tok-tok drive or a two-hour walk away, during the wet season.

After inspecting the local penned pigs and free-range chooks, turkeys and ducks, we make it out into the rice fields. A crop is planted in June, at the beginning of the wet season and harvested, by hand in December, before the hot season withers it.

Then on a further couple of hundred metres to the village wat: in reality just a rather dilapidated wooden house with a large verandah. The outside walls are painted with very simple illustrations of the Buddha's life. There is one middle-aged monk and two novices, both under ten years of age who are young lads from the village.

Chanthy is keen to show Iain the water-driven method for generating electricity; a tiny turning mechanism placed in a hand constructed water sluice off the edge of the small river that runs beside the village. OK in the wet season, but useless in the long dry, when water has to be hand carried from the dwindling river by hand or raised from wells.

A better system is needed.

Back in the village we are informed it is time for an evening bathe in the river, along with all the other villagers. This turned out to be very refreshing and fun too, with a lot of splashing and laughing.

Then half an hour later, dressed in our travel worn best, borrowed scarves draped across our hearts and surrounded by several dozen assorted relatives plus the village headman, teacher and other notables, the basi ceremony gets underway with us as guests of honour.

This basi ceremony is no less thought provoking and spine-tingling than on the first occasion we had encountered it, but because that only happened a few chapters back I'll pick up from where, after it has been performed and a simple meal eaten, an animated discussion started up among the villagers.

The conversation according to Chanthy who translated the gist of the talk, was all about the coming of electricity to the village, due at the year's end. It was still going on and Chanthy's parents, who were no longer wearing any of their basi finery had begun to look decidedly as if they would like their guests to leave, but were too polite to say so, when Iain and my systems go into shut down mode and we just lie down against the wall and fall into a deep sleep!

At dawn, woken by choruses from cockerels and dogs, we are up and having freshened ourselves from a bowl of water set aside for us, have already been served fried eggs by Chanthy. He is absolutely determined that this is what we would want to eat because he's seen hundreds of *falangs* eat this for breakfast every day at the riverside cafe where he works.

Later, we face the toils of the return tok-tok trip. This machine being the latest model, a four-geared Thai beauty, makes lighter work of the journey than the previous one had. But added to by yesterday's heavy downpour the mud is now some many centimeters deeper. At one point we have to stop to help extricate another tok-tok that has become bogged while carrying a small child and his anxious mother on a journey to Muang Nan District Hospital. At the river, Thongkhan and Buachanh wave us off and it is with a quietly heart-sore, homesick Chanthy we travel back up against the strong current of the Mekong to Luang Prabang.

Looking back now on that occasion it is our final view of Buachanh and Thongkhan standing on the muddy bank of the Mekong waving us goodbye that we remember most strongly.

Thoughts about inequality, redistribution of resources, fate, luck, opportunity, hammer at us as we, like Chanthy, sit quietly in the boat as it struggles upstream against the massive current.

'It's the road,' Iain speaks that night into the dark, instinctively aware that I too am lying there mulling over what we have experienced. 'There's so much they need. Electricity. Water storage. Gutters. Solar panels. A clinic. Regular visits by a doctor or a nurse.

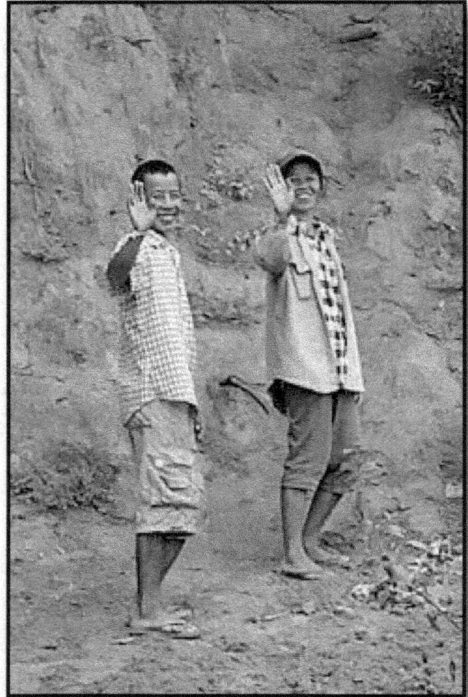

Chanthy s parents:
Thongkhan and Buachanh

It goes on. But it's the road. The road is key.'

The very next day after our return from NaLin, call it fate, call it serendipity, whatever, at our regular breakfast café we spot a Frenchman we have met in passing at the home of an Australian couple whom we knew from our volunteering days in Vietnam.

We know that Florent Le Fabre is the local manager of a medium-sized French construction and plant leasing company, RMA. So on the premise of nothing ventured, nothing gained, we go across to the table, where Florent, a rather handsome man, is obviously enjoying the company of a visiting trio of chic young French women. We ask him if we can drop by his office for a chat about a project we are planning.

At this stage we don't have anything even remotely resembling a project or a plan, but that is how the words came out. Perhaps the fact we speak to him in French helps. You know how the French are about their language. A time is arranged and it is during this meeting a day later, that Florent tells us the generally estimated cost of building a simple road in Laos with a compacted, but not sealed surface. Depending, *naturelement*, on the terrain and whether or not there is a need for bridges; 'Around $10,000 per kilometre,' he says.

We have already estimated the distance from the Mekong to NaLin to be in the region of five kilometers, give or take a bit. So, making allowances for this and that, perhaps a good, but rough guestimate for what we have already started calling The Road to NaLin would be $60,000. It is at least a ballpark figure. And really it doesn't seem to be too fantastically unobtainable. Does it?

In another of what we take to be good signs, over a farewell dinner with that same couple of Australian ex-volunteers, Greg Blake and Evi Czernechi, it is mentioned, in a passing response to our idea about the possibility of building a Road to NaLin, that the Australian Ambassador to Laos has at her personal disposal varying amounts of funding in annual grants under a system called the Direct Aid Programme. They suggest we should apply for one. We know it is too early but we file the idea away for future reference.

The last few days are inundated with a snowstorm of paperwork. Chanthy wants to change schools from the one he has attended all this present scholastic year to one he is now certain, from conversations he's had with other students, has higher educational demands and standards. But to do that he needs to obtain a certificate from his former school confirming that he has attended and what grades he has obtained. He is not at all sure how to go about this but we tell him that a copy of his leaving certificate is his by right, though we have no idea if this is in fact correct. When he appears still nervous about the suggestion that he should just front up there and request a copy of his enrolment and the grades he has obtained, we say we'll come with him. That is all the encouragement he needs.

We have to keep reminding ourselves that here is a young man, a boy in Australian terms, the first person from his village to leave in order to further his education, but still a country kid in the big city. As it turns out it is indeed just as straightforward as we had hoped it might be.

Another official hurdle is the need for a photo ID that has to be presented at the local police station. Forms are required stating that Chanthy Sisombuth will be residing in Luang Prabang for a year longer than his original application stated. This is also not too difficult because as Chanthy puts it, 'I have a cousin in the police.'

But no short cuts are open to us for his enrolment at the new college, the Teachers Training College (TTC). Even though the teaching staff, including the Principal, who turns out to be Australian trained, all assume we have come along ourselves to join the teaching faculty and are disappointed when we explain, me with a huge degree of relief, that we are not teachers. It takes almost a half a day to fill in the various forms and walk around the large campus searching for the correct offices in which to drop these off. Fees are not being accepted until a few weeks later.

This means there is one more official bear to confront: the bank. We want Chanthy to open an account so he can deposit these fees, plus a little bit extra for emergencies, rather than needing to keep the monies on his person.

The talk we gave Chanthy about banking would make our own bank manager's eyes water and is pretty odd coming from people who are none too smart with their own money, probably because we regard money as just one aspect of life, not a central focus.

Once all that is sorted there is one more necessary stop: a shop-up at Phosi Market. Here we trail around after Chanthy as he tries on the regulation clothing for those who attend TTC. One pair of black trousers, two white long-sleeved shirts, and a pair of black lace-up shoes. That is it. Chanthy doesn't ask for anything extra.

I love my children. I even loved them when they were teenagers. But it is a different sort of pleasure to shop with Chanthy! There is absolutely no pressure to buy brand names, though I have to admit there are none available at Phosi Market.

Even when it comes to choosing a light jacket to wear in the early mornings of the cooler months, Chanthy knows what he needs rather than what he wants. The same applies to his choice of a sturdy shoulder bag in which to carry his schoolbooks and notepads. These last we also stock up on along with pencils and pens.

'All done,' he announces as we are leaving the market by tuk-tuk, with whose driver he bargains to pay the usual local charge rather than the increased fare because two *falang* are aboard.

'Thank you Dear Iain Dear Trish,' Chanthy says with grace and having learnt, 'Thank you Chanthy,' we reply.

We send some monies to our longtime Sydney pal Dave Best and suggesting some guidelines, ask him to choose three photographic books about Australia and to send them up to us.

Because ever since we had first met him Chanthy has expressed a fascination for deep water, his book is about the oceans surrounding Australia and the extraordinary life to which they are home. With our novice friend, Khamchanh we have talked about the tectonic plates and land bridges that made it possible for Australian flora and fauna to develop independently so his book is about the indigenous animals and plants unique to the continent. To Thiemchanh and Noi, because of their instinctive appreciation of beauty, expressed in the careful detailing in their home we give an artistic, photographic essay containing a variety of Australian landscapes. We have perhaps never given gifts that have given us so much pleasure.

Chanthy comes to see us off, this time at the airport, where he has never been before. He standsby the wire fence watching in silent intensity as the plane comes in from Bangkok. Then he turns to us and asks, 'What is it like in a plane when it flies into cloud?'

He wants to wait until we are called to board. Then he stands, still a little stiffly and lets first Iain and then me hug him goodbye.

'Oh Chanthy,' I say, noticing for the first time and babbling in an effort to cover my emotions, 'you have your new school shoes on.'

He smiles and nods. 'This is my first ever pair of real shoes.'

9

FITTING BACK IN

When you hear the words, Culture Shock, the picture instantly conjured up is of an Australian, or other Westerner being overwhelmed by the sounds, smells and sights of Asia, perhaps in particular, by the press of people.

But for us it often works in reverse. Leaving Asia and coming home the shock is the lack of people; at nine o'clock at night, where is everyone? How old everyone is and how large. Realising that we are all these things also is cause for extra shock. One of the more unnerving aspects is being able to understand the multitude of casual conversations that go on all around us. It seems like so much chatter.

We find ourselves trying to avoid shops, especially malls, with their excessive amount of product for sale. Everything seems to cost an exorbitant amount of money. That's relative to what we've been experiencing, I know, but people look affluent and living standards are apparently rising. All of which is okay, well almost okay, but we experience an underlying uncomfortable feeling that the economics are out of whack; that we, Australians, have too much, while others close by, have too little; that there needs to be a fairer distribution of available resources.

But daily swims in our ocean creek, the fresh, light tang of the air, the high blue sky, the generous hospitality of friends, the pungent smell of the eucalypts and the extraordinarily crystalline light mean we are home and happy to be so.

Also Christmas is coming which means school holidays, lots of visitors and no time for moping around. The annual round up of news has to be sent out with home-produced Season's Greetings cards. Though quite quickly a real seesaw of emotions begins to take over as we begin telling people about Chanthy, Khamchanh, Thiemchanh, NaLin and our plans for The Road.

One long time friend assures us that the building of a road will open the village to prostitution and drugs. In similar vein another comments that a road will destroy the villagers' way of life. Yet another suggests that Chanthy is wily and sees us merely as an ATM on legs. While one more asks us what we personally will get out of the project. A family member asks, 'why doesn't their government build them a road?'

I learn that people's initial response is their truest. Later they can dissemble and pfaff politely but I'm convinced their first comments remain what they actually think.

As a counter to these comments we are very glad to receive a phone call from Stephen Midgley in Canberra. We had literally bumped into Stephen's Laos-born wife, Dao on our penultimate day in Luang Prabang in, of all places, a very small-scale equivalent of Bunnings Hardware store. We were searching for washers and nuts to replace a security device Iain had fitted to both our travel pulley bags. Dao wanted paint, large quantities of it.

'For my school.' She spoke as if we would be aware of this facility, then realizing we were not, immediately told us she and her husband Stephen have built a bridge, housing for a number of Hmong families, a small wat and that very day, 'we are having a blessing ceremony for our school, you must come, it is not far outside town and the Australian Ambassador is coming.'

Dao is very attractive, has a soft Australian accent and a large, warm personality with which she envelops all who meet her. Stephen, 'when I saw him, I fell in love with him immediately,' she told us, 'is the most handsome, loving man in the world.' He is an agronomist. They visit Laos at least three times a year because Stephen has on-going work commitments there as well as in Vietnam and China. They also have a home and an adult daughter, Malou, in Canberra.

That is from where Stephen is calling now. We had told Dao of our nascent road project and later written an email to her expanding on our ideas. Down the phone Stephen is cheerfully supportive.

'You will of course need to be there when the road is built,' he cautioned,' or bags of cement will sprout legs.'

We agree, but tell him there is a long road to travel before we get to that point. 'But from the very beginning' he cautioned, 'you need someone on the ground whom you can trust. A Lao.' We tell him about Chanthy and say we will send them material about the project as it develops and that we would like to come down to Canberra to meet up sometime during the coming year. He closes his call by saying, 'Thank you for caring.'

While in Luang Prabang we couldn't attend the opening of the Midgley's new school, but we realised not long after, that in Dao we had encountered a member of what we eventually came to call The Laos Underground. The phone chat with Stephen confirmed that.

We keep up to speed with what is happening in Laos by reading a daily dose of the on-line newspaper Lao Voices. It is of course a government-run outlet and as such the 'news' is always positive, oftentimes hilariously so, unless it's about Thailand.

Late in December, while house and cat sitting for friends in Sydney, we visit the offices of the Liquor, Gaming and Racing Board, recently euphemistically rebadged as Communities NSW. Here we apply in person for a Fundraising Authority to the Manager: Charities Licensing, Steve Blackburn.

The forms are a bit daunting but, as we have often enjoined Chanthy, the mantra is: Step-by-Step, Bit-by-Bit.

There is a requirement in obtaining this authority to form a committee of at least three people, no two of which may cohabit; such coy language. We ask two friends, fellow residents of the upper Tweed Valley, entertainment entrepreneur Phil Bathols and businessman Marty Rubenstein, to join the venture and they both willingly agree; Phil as Treasurer, Marty as Secretary. Iain is Chairman.

We head back up to our home in northern NSW with our grandchildren for a few days break for them away from Sydney, but are shortly marooned for a couple of days by rising flood waters, while nearby Brisbane suffers a major flood disaster.

On the day they fly out of Brisbane, to go back home, there is a full-scale alert at the airport with talk of it being closed due to dangerous floodwaters. For them however, it's an adventure. Macs comments that this is the first real-life drama, as distinct from television pretend dramas, he has ever experienced. They want to get back to their parents and their mates, but even so they are somewhat disappointed that the incoming plane makes it through the continuing torrents, turns around and they are carried away into the deluge.

As for us, we can now hunker down at our computers. Iain begins to edit together some nonprofessional stills and footage he has shot in Laos that could be used as a visual presentation in an as yet unknown situation. I write a background piece on Laos, also with as wide an appeal as possible.

We have very quickly discovered that Laos is not a name that springs quickly to mind for many people the majority of whom has no real idea where it is. Some are even unsure what it is. Even those who know it is a country somewhere in south east Asia are reluctant to try to pronounce the name. President Kennedy, with all those resources at his beck and call, managed to mangle it as Lay-os, and that at a time when the USA was bombing the bejesus out of the place.

On the assumption that people are not going to give over their hard earned monies to help people in a place they only have the most vague notion about, we include information about the geography, history, politics, social structure, economy and religion of Laos.

We show it all, the video and the hard copy to Phil, who is slightly more than half our age and in tune with the ways of the Internet. 'Very interesting,' he says politely. 'But what I need to show to people is a grabber, two minutes at most, preferably less. People,' he assures us, 'don't have time for all that information.' He doesn't even flick through the hard copy.

We show it all, the video and the hard copy, to Marty and he suggests we approach the Rotary Club of Murwillumbah. He's not a member there but he knows people who are. 'I'll ask around,' he says.

Without looking at it he holds on to a hard copy, 'to show other people', he says.

Other suggestions are that we look at using Crowdfunding and Kickstarter, both web-based methods of raising money for projects. We are confronted by what is, to me in particular, a new world and one I admit to feeling uncomfortable about. The one common consensus is that we need to get the story out on Youtube and Facebook. It would seem that absolutely nothing happens unless it happens on Youtube.

We can't go public until we get approval from Communities NSW and we have been told that may take up to six weeks. It's a chicken and egg situation. Meanwhile Iain begins to edit together a short version of an appeal.

On the roller-coaster ride that The Road to NaLin has already become we suddenly get an email from Chanthy asking us to phone him. It sounds urgent.

We stand on the front deck of our place looking down over the dams, that are now brimming with rainfall and listen to him disconsolately tell us, 'I have left my job.'

In the final few days of our stay in Luang Prabang we had met with a middle-aged Western woman at whose riverside restaurant we had eaten on numerous occasions. Over the months we had pieced together a little of her life-story; the fact that she had two very young children and that it was

96

quite obvious from their colouring and features that they had different fathers, already indicated that she was a risk-taker and had lived the life. Good on her. Who wouldn't want to swap her native land's killing winters for the tropical beauty and warmth of Laos?

Her restaurant caters mostly for tourists and just recently has seen a big increase in the number of those coming from China. She was also on the point of stretching her resources to their limit in order to open a second venue. She was looking for staff. We quizzed her on what she paid and the conditions under which her staff operated.

It all sounded pretty good, with a better wage than Chanthy was getting at Khonkhai and with professional training given in how to mix drinks, how to approach and deal with customers, how to sell meals and front of house operations as well as behind the scenes procedures.

We told Chanthy about what we saw as an opportunity for him to climb a rung or two up the employment ladder He was nervous about being interviewed for the position but we did some interview role-playing with him, talked up his abilities and self-confidence and off he'd gone to meet the restaurateur and been immediately offered the job. He had been delighted.

But in his call to us now, after a couple of months in the job, he sounds downcast. 'I am sorry DearTrishDearIain but I have to tell you that,' he mentions his boss's name, 'she wants me to love her.'

We have the speakerphone on so both of us can hear and respond, but we are left speechless at this. There is a pause.

'What did she...?' Iain begins.

Chanthy interrupts: 'But I cannot. I cannot love her. She is much older than me,' We can sense his incredulity. 'and she has already two children.'

Ah. There was the rub: Chanthy's comments were clearly code for the fact that the behind-the-scenes procedures at the restaurant turned out to include rather more than anticipated. Which just goes to show what poor judges of character we are. We felt like such utter fools. How embarrassing for Chanthy to have to rebuff the unwanted advances of his boss. But how glad we were he was able to tell us, albeit obtusely, what had happened.

We apologize to him for the behaviour of his boss and explain how we feel responsible for him being placed in that awkward position and to thank him for telling us what had happened. Knowing how meagre his financial margin is, we start making noises about there being other jobs and that we are sure he will find another one soon.

'I already have a new job,' he announces. 'I wait to get a new job before I tell you. This one is in a shop. It sells ethnic clothing and other things made by mountain people.'

Obviously a steep learning curve will need to be negotiated. But we are delighted that Chanthy has secured a position as a salesman in an up-market boutique specializing in clothing and handmade products created by Hmong, Khmu, Ahka, as well as other minority people.

He tells us the name of the shop, Kopnoi and is pleased we know where it is, that it means 'little frog' and that we have been there.

We ask with some trepidation, 'Who owns the shop?' He mangles her very French name, 'She's very nice lady,' then adds, '...and old, much older.' The three of us laugh, with shared relief.

10

FIRST DONATION

A week later Laos has a sudden burst of notoriety in Australia; unfortunately not for happy reasons but for horror and sadness. It was due to an Australian television screening of a film made in 2008 by the German director Marc Eberle, titled *The Most Secret Place on Earth*.

The film is an in your face retelling of the horrific bombing of an officially neutral Laos by the US that dropped some two millions tonnes of ordnance on the country from 1964 to 1973 during the Vietnam War. In 580,000 bombing missions, the equivalent of a planeload of bombs every 8 minutes, 24 hours a day every day for 9 years, Laos became the most heavily bombed country per capita in history.

Those calmly stated statistics come from the carefully measured tones of the *Legacies of War* website and refer to not just what might be described as 'regular' ordnance, that is bombs, but also napalm and Agent Orange. They are perhaps the main reason why Laos stays below the mental radar of the majority of Westerners on the premise that it is easier to misremember, code for forget, unpleasant facts and recall only the good times.

Many of the pilots who flew these murderous raids were actually mercenaries, former US air force pilots, technically not employed by the military, wearing civilian clothes and paid much more than regular air force pilots. They were also acting far beyond the boundaries of the United Nations rules of engagement. Presidents Eisenhower, Kennedy, Nixon and Ford all lied to their people at home, as well as to the entire world, about the non-stop bombing in Laos. While the existence of Long Chen, the mountain stronghold from which these men flew in planes owned and operated by the CIA, was being continuously denied, Long Chen grew to be the world's busiest airport.

In a bizarrely twisted manner *The Most Secret Place on Earth* gave some credibility to a number of the things we had been trying to get across about the plight of the country. Another positive outcome was that it at least succeeded in bringing Laos to the front of peoples' mental map.

Around the same time, a more concrete and positive representation of this arrived in the mail from Communities NSW: our vital Charitable Fundraising Authority. We had become number CFN/21888. *The Road to NaLin Fund* was now legal.

In the manner of country living, the Bush Telegraph begins to hum and Marty Rubenstein's inquiries about Rotary bring about an invitation for us to address one of their regular weekly meetings.

So the net widens and everyone we know, plus their cousins and their cousin's great-nieces, becomes grist for our Laos mill! Emails, those curses and blessings, zoom off into space and zoom back landing in electronic in-trays around the world.

Our immediate search focuses down to looking for an engineer. We discover that 2011 has been designated the Year of the Humanitarian Engineer. What is more, the young man chosen as Engineer of the Year, Chris McGrath, is a young Australian who has been working in Laos! It takes a few phone calls and emails to track him down but when we do, it is to a high-rise office in Sydney, where he is now employed. He agrees to meet next time we are down on house/cat-sitting duties.

When we do eventually get together I sense that Chris is also suffering from intermittent waves of reverse Culture Shock. He would really like to help, he says, to go back to Laos, which he misses a lot, but he is a Water not a Road or Civil Engineer, which is what we need. He suggests we try Engineers Without Borders, the engineering schools of the universities and big engineering companies. In particular, he mentions SMEC, formerly the Snowy Mountains Electricity Commission, responsible for building the huge Snowy Mountains Electricity scheme that employed many thousands of what were then described as New Australians.

Now designated as the Snowy Mountains Engineering Corporation, the company has offices in many parts of the world but in particular in south east Asia. 'They seem to have a bit of heart,' Chris comments. We later take his advice and ring the company headquarters. We are told to look up their website and if we feel we fit within their guidelines, to download their grant application forms, fill them in and send them to their Melbourne office.

'Good luck,' Chris says as he shakes our hands in farewell, 'Keep in touch' and in an echo of Stephen Midgley says ' Thank you,' not as a form of superficial politeness, but as an expression of a shared bond of caring.

On a mild sunny day, with Bondi Beach showing off to full the tantalizing allure of its Emerald City beauty, we meet with filmmaker Mark Gould who has come into our lives through Phil Bathols, Treasurer of our Road to NaLin committee. Mark shoots footage of many of the concerts and other entertainments that Phil presents on stage.

Now he shoots a couple of pieces to camera with Iain and I using Bondi as a magnificent backdrop, to contrast the difference in lifestyle between people here and those struggling with conditions in NaLin.

We draw up a Time Line and a SWOT analysis. Alongside these I pin a worksheet, designating jobs to people we know whom we think would best perform these necessary and related tasks. There is also a list of potential sources of financial and/or hands on support. Yes, its all a bit fanciful but it helps to print these out and pin them up above our work desks, in line of sight, as constant concrete reminders of what needs to be done in order to achieve our goal of completing The Road to NaLin project that has begun to swallow our lives!

To finally finish the six-minute video Iain needs a shot of an engineer at work and through the expanding RNL network we meet Josh Neale. Meeting people such as Josh is just one of the many great pluses of the task we have undertaken. Immediately helpful and totally understanding of what it is we need and are up to, he allows Iain to shoot a short piece in the office of his small engineering company that overlooks the ocean creek where we do our laps every day.

With a sixth sense, we get the feeling that there is a back story to Josh, who is perhaps in his early thirties, married and who, with a little prodding reveals that a couple of years back he joined with a group of other young Australian professionals who spent three months in Calcutta where they built a school. 'Nothing flash,' he wants us to know, 'very basic but functional. I loved doing it. It was...,' he raises his hands to chest level, palms up, in a gesture of inadequacy, 'such a small thing to do in the face of all that is needed. But the people there were delighted and I was even more so. I want to go back and do more.'

We quiz him on how the school-building project was initiated. 'Through my church,' he told us. I am beginning to understand that the Laos Underground has branches everywhere.

With the last piece of the video jigsaw finally in place and wanting to ensure there will be no technical glitches, we arrange with the owner/operators of the riverside restaurant where Murwillumbah Rotary hold their meetings to come by on the morning of the day of the evening get together. We check out their equipment, carrying with us an assortment of jacks, leads and extension cords. Iain's six-minute story comes up well on the restaurant's extra big screen. Everything is spot on. We can relax, we think.

That evening as the setting sun glistens on the river the men assemble for pre-dinner drinks on the restaurant's wide verandah. There is male banter and they are courteous to me in that old-fashioned gentlemanly manner that has gone out of style, but which I appreciate.

Rotary, a service club established in 1905 in the USA now has 32,000 clubs worldwide and a membership of 1.2million. Its basic principle, of putting service before self, is of course admirable. But ask around among your friends and I'm betting you will discover it is in serious need of a large-scale, public relations makeover to freshen up an image that remains one of elderly Anglo-Saxon conservative-minded men with time on their hands doing good works. In fact it is far more than that.

We are called inside to dinner at a horseshoe-shaped seating arrangement where a sort of teasing repartee gets underway. The emcee for the evening imposes 'fines' for supposed and mischievously manufactured misbehaviours. All this carry-on is a mix of American Freshman college ritual and British Scouts palaver. In Australian terms it's a mateship ritual.

We are introduced, thanked for coming and the meals are served. I introduce myself to the man sitting beside me who comments on the fact that my plate is placed in front of me ahead of everyone else's. 'Aah,' I wisecrack in an unguarded manner, 'that's not because I am a woman, it's because I am vegetarian,' and with that, we're off and running, the chat hopping from subject to subject.

Murray Franks is a very easy man with whom to converse. He also presents as different from all the other Rotarians in the room. He is a less conservative dresser, indeed he's rather flash. He wears a gold watch, chains and rings, one of which holds a large, semi-precious, stone. He is affable, self-assured and charming.

He asks why I am vegetarian and I give him my smartarse response that 'I'm actually a 'vegaquarian' I eat fish, 'for my brain,' but then do a bit of a rant about not needing to eat hard-hoofed beasts who destroy the Australian landscape.

'What about chicken?'

'Oh no,' I assure him adamantly, 'chickens are fed so many antibiotics they are dangerous to eat.'

He raises his eyebrows and nods thoughtfully.

He asks about The Road, the poverty in Laos and as he seems genuinely interested, I go on to talk about Chanthy as an explanation of how we became involved with the project to build a road to NaLin and finish up by assuring him what a quantum difference it will make to the lives of the three hundred villagers.

I was so busy trying to draw him on side, I didn't stop once to ask if he had been to Laos or to anywhere else in south east Asia.

He asks where we live and after painting a picture of a rural idyll, I ask him where he lives. 'On the twentieth floor of an apartment block in Surfers Paradise.' He smiles engagingly. 'I don't do trees.'

'But at least you have a beautiful ocean beach,' I say brightly.

'Nor beaches, oceans or swimming,' he assures me.

OK then. A pause as I mentally juggle with that information before asking, 'So as you live in Surfers, why drive forty minutes to come down to a Rotary Club in Murwillumbah .

'Because I am here a couple of days a week to keep an eye on my business,' he explains with noticeable humour in his voice.

'What sort of business is that?'

'We grow and process chickens for market.'

I must have blinked or gulped, at least I like to think that in my tactlessness I did. But right at that moment the emcee taps his glass with a fork, asks Iain and I to make our presentation and matters go from bad to worse.

Iain gives some background to The Road project. I add my bit, though most of my brain is still reeling from my social gaffe. Iain throws the switch and the screen bursts into life, with static. Pause, much fiddling with wires and connections. He tries again. Static once more fills the screen. The restaurant owner is called upon. Neither he nor Iain, nor any of the assorted others who try, can fix the problem, or even know what the problem is. Iain keeps babbling about it working perfectly well during this morning's trial. I keep smiling and chatting on about what they would be seeing if only the machines would work.

After an interminable time, during which Iain has begun to sweat profusely, we decide to show the video on the much smaller screen of his laptop computer. He stands apologizing, at the mouth of the seated horseshoe and holds the computer in his hands out towards the assembled men, while I wonder what else can go wrong.

When it is over, the men clap politely, a couple of them ask questions and I find that Murray Franks has come up beside me and is holding out, what is this? Can it possibly be a cheque? It is. A blank cheque for $1000!

'You fill in the name,' he suggests. 'And good luck with The Road. My girlfriend is Thai, she comes from a village just like NaLin.' I give him a big hug and try to apologize for my rudeness but he won't hear a word of it.

'What you had to say was very interesting,' he fibbs politely.

The following day, armed with the official license from Communities NSW we open The Road to Na Lin Fund bank account at the Commonwealth Bank in Murwillumbah. Both Phil and Marty are present in order to make it all above board and Phil asks if the Bank makes special concessions for charities.

'There will be no bank fees charged', the smiling clerk assures us.

I fill in the name on the cheque and we bank our first donation to the fund, Murray Franks' $1000. Then, certain this is an auspicious start to our fundraising, we cross the road to have a celebratory coffee.

11

VIDEOS/YOUTUBE/WEBSITE

Around this time The Road to NaLin begins to really take over our lives.

Our first official Committee Meeting takes place, over dinner at our home. I keep the minutes and later send them out for Marty and Phil to sign. Phil mentions the possibility of organizing a fundraising concert and also confidently assures us that 'Surely living the life you have, you must know sixty people who would give a thousand dollars each.' We are gob-smacked by this suggestion. But laying awake that night and bearing in mind Murray Franks' generous donation of $1000, I think maybe Phil's got a point. Having lived this long and thus having met a vast number of people from across the social spectrum, surely we must know sixty people who will give us a thousand dollars. Just goes to show how vaingloriously wrong one can be!

Chanthy calls from Laos. Pi Mai time has come around again and in a cheerfully uplifting conversation, he tells us that this year he will be given time off work to enjoy the festivities. He is looking forward to experiencing the same fun Iain and I had the previous year.

He has other news:he is going to briefly become a novice in the Sibounheung Wat in Muang Nan District, near where he attended high school. His parents and brother and sister, plus aunts and cousins will present him to the abbot of the wat. They will need to make a donation, a small amount of cash and simple goods, to the wat. He will have his head and eyebrows shaved, put on the orange robes and live the life of a novice.

Even though his stay in the wat will last for only three days, this is an extremely significant occasion in his life. Every young Lao man aspires to do this before he marries. This is not school camp or Outward Bound; it reverberates deeply with giving honour and receiving an honouring. Chanthy will be the first male in his family to do this, thus earning merit, not only for his entire clan, but according to Lao tradition, for his mother in particular. He is excited though nervous.

We assure him that he will be a good representative of his family and that, in our terms, he will do them proud.

He asks whether there are wats in Australia. When we tell him yes, he is surprised and asks if there are also monks and is even more surprised when we again say yes. It is unnecessary, we think, to go further and explain to him that Buddhism in Australia is mostly of the 'other sect'. Buddhism is

Buddhism like Christianity is Christianity. But perhaps only outsiders see it like that. As always, Laos raises questions.

We carry our computers everywhere and show whoever wants as well no doubt as a great many who do not, our videos that now include a mini version for people with short attention spans. Iain works on getting up The Road to NaLin website in the hope that this will attract donors.

For a brief period, we allow ourselves to get side tracked into renovating the garden shed, as one does. It's a great relief to have this hands-on work to balance up the many hours spent at the computers. We saw and screw, hammer and paint. We lay an extra layer of secondhand tin on the roof to stop the leaks; stuff the ceiling and walls with insulation then line them all and make shelving. Visits to Bunnings Warehouse are so frequent; the staff knows us by name and joke with us about being 'late to work today.'

All these renos tend to play havoc with our knees and a bright, too-young surgeon cheerfully informs both of us that we have, 'arthritic deterioration due to age'. I sourly tell him that, if he is lucky, this will happen to him too and Iain goes in for stopgap day surgery to have his knee joint cleaned up.

During his enforced recuperation Iain's self-created The Road to NaLin website springs into life. We open a bottle of champagne to sip as we sit on our deck and celebrate.

On the day we send our website details out to friends and foes alike we also receive an email from Khamchanh letting us know that it is Buddha's Birthday. It is also Buddha's Deathday and thus also the Day of his Attainment.

Robin Taylor, who was the impetus for our visit to Laos, responds to our emailed website details to inform us that friends of her cousin are also involved in raising funds for Laos. We now immediately recognize the sign for the Laos Underground and call these people, Robyn and John Salisbury who live not far from us at Mt. Tambourine, just across the border in Queensland. They invite us to visit.

It is such a pleasure and relief to be with people to whom there is no need for explanations. With Robyn and John we can have shorthand conversations. They have been spending time in Laos for over a decade and have built a road. Yes a road! And what is more they have built a bridge, a sizeable one, across a real river and also a school; all of this in the village of Houy Phand in the northern part of Luang Prabang Province.

They have accomplished these improvements with monies they have raised independently in their small community in the beautiful high hills behind the Gold Coast. It gladdens our hearts and makes The Road to NaLin seem possible.

In addition Robyn, who runs a hairdressing business from a salon that is part of their home and

John, who is a builder have sponsored a young man, their 'heart-son', Bounmee who is now in his mid thirties and is working with John in his business.

His younger sister, Oun, has now joined Bounmee, who had spent most of his life living as a novice in a village wat when the Salisburys came into his life. Keeping it all in the family Oun is about to marry the Salisbury's godson.

Bounmee and Oun make dinner for us all; good home-cooked Lao food and we all talk, with a degree of fervour about Laos and our dreams for what we want to do there.

'I do get homesick,' Bounmee tells us. 'But I have an unbelievably better life here. All I need is a Lao wife. Yes,' he told us in response to our probing, 'I have dated Australian girls and they are very nice but,' he pauses and we know he is thinking how to put this politely, 'I think it will be better for me to marry a Lao girl because there is a big difference in the way of doing things.'

We take the plunge into a world we have resisted and Iain manages to put both his RNL videos, the six-minute and the two-minute versions, up on YouTube. It doesn't go viral. But we do receive a enough responses to be a daily challenge.

Chanthy asks in an email if we could help him with the rent for a room of his own. He has been sleeping for over a year on a roll out mattress at an uncle's little house, paying a small amount as board and keep and helping out by getting up early in order to prepare the day's rice, as well as going to the morning market to buy the daily food needs for the family. We discuss rent and conditions for a room he has found close to his college and make suggestions, such as asking the landlord for a month's free accommodation in exchange for paying a year's rent in advance.

It is a miniature room in a long row of similar rooms. He explains that these are mostly rented out to students, who all share the two loos and the outside washing area. He tells us his sister Bounlee is coming to join him in Luang Prabang and that she hopes to be accepted at the same college he is attending, only she will study to become a kindergarten teacher.

Our lives teeter between commitments in Laos and the New South Wales Northern Rivers area.

We are asked again if we can house-cat-sit for our friends in Sydney, Brent Waters and Margaret Gee for a short period while they pay one of their regular visits to Bhutan, where Brent, who is a forensic psychiatrist, is gradually establishing a small clinic on a voluntary basis. The Laos Underground clearly operates in places other than Laos. In addition, as it is school holidays, we can be useful in that area of our son's hectic family life.

Driving down to Sydney, we pick up granddaughter Milla and drive on to Canberra, where we spend a few days enjoying the terrific science museum, Questacom, as well as taking the opportunity of meeting up with Laos

Undergrounders Dao and Stephen Midgley and their daughter Malou.

Over the last decade Dao and Stephen have built not one or even two but three schools, plus a small and significantly beautiful wat and a village water supply and toilet block as well as assisting a growing number of young people through the equivalent of TAFE professional courses in fields as diverse as engineering and hairdressing. Dao also specialises in projects to assist village women set up small businesses particularly appliqué embroidery.

Before we leave them to head off back to Sydney, both Dao and Stephen give us a piece of important advice. 'You must have a letter, written in Lao and signed by the village headman, saying that they and all the people of the village want you to build The Road to NaLin. This letter must have a red chop, the official seal of the local branch of the Communist Party. Two preferably. In fact the more chops the better!'

Back in Sydney Iain updates the blog for the Road to NaLin website and has fruitless conversations with people at SMEC, the former Snowy Mountains Electricity Commission. At the same time Janet Brennand and Dick Sheppard come to stay with us after spending a year on a teaching assignment on the Indonesian island of Lombok. They have travelled home via Luang Prabang where they stayed at Khoumxiengthong Guesthouse with Noi and Thiemchanh's family. They also met up with our novice friend Khamchanh as well as of course with Chanthy, so we get first hand reports of how everyone there is going.

Franz Xaver Augustine, a good friend from our time in Vietnam who is now based in Djakarta and runs the Goethe Institute for the whole of south east Asia, from the Philippines to India, Australia and New Zealand, visits and we of course talk about The Road to NaLin. This leads to a discovery about Franz Xaver that we had not known before. He too is part of the Laos Underground, only his Laos is in India, where together with a group of friends he has built and continues to fund a secondary school for girls.

There is a growing understanding that the world would not operate, even as erratically as it does now, without a wide web of people doing their bit to support it. If we relied solely on governments, the world would more than likely tip off its axis, over weighted with greed and hubris.

Back home after our sojourn in Sydney, a huge storm envelops us in roaring wind, thunderclaps, and finally drenching rain. Outdoor furniture is thrown around. We brave the main deck but there is nothing we can do in the face of such furies. Sheet lightening illuminates the range on the far side of the crater of the extinct volcano that usually forms our distant view. We hear small trees and branches from larger ones, cracking and crashing.

For the following two days the phone is not

operating and so we also have no Internet connection. I find this a relief. When connections are restored the very first email we open is from Chanthy sending photographs of his brother Jai's wedding to his village sweetheart, Binh.

Jai and Binh's wedding

Jai had spent more than a year working on the buses but come to the conclusion that it was not the life for him, so he had come home to the village with other plans.

His wedding, like all others in Laos, had to be a big affair and because the groom's family, by custom, must foot the bill, placed a colossal burden on the Sisombuth family, which had to borrow money for the wedding.

A couple of weeks later we hand over *Amungula*, which is the name of our bit of land and which means *Place Where The Little Birds Sing*, to long time friends and both widows, Gerda Menzel and Christa Weikl.

Without even being asked and without even telling us she had done so Gerda had put a thousand dollars into The Road account; this at a time when we really needed the boost of having friends who believed in us. Christa also made a generous donation and now they kindly offer to come up north to stay in our house, while we are away from Australia. For them it is also a chance to escape the Adelaide winter.

Then we head off once again to Laos.

12

NALIN AGAIN

The two weeks we now spend in Laos are crammed to the edges with events and happenings, all of them positive. It is so good to be back. Reading back through my diary I sense a relaxed feeling but also one of anticipation of an incredible adventure to come of which more shortly.

In the capital, Vientiane, we visit the government mapping office and get good quality large-scale maps of NaLin and Muang Nan district. With a touch of paranoia we had been concerned beforehand that in a country that still has sizeable areas closed both to its own people and to foreigners, there would be queries about why we wanted these maps. But Ms. Chanthone

Vientiane Mapping Office

Piokeopaseuth, the cartographer in charge of the department, could not have been more helpful.

At Luang Prabang airport we are unexpectedly met by Noi, as if by a family member. Back at the Khoumxiengthong guesthouse, Thiemchanh has a bowl of delicious noodle soup ready for us. Pampered.

An excited and pleased Chanthy shows up and we go shopping for some basic stuff for his room. At the Phosi Market we purchase an electric fan, a plastic water jug, a set of plastic coated wire shelves and a woven plastic floor mat. We leave it to Chanthy to make the choices and to bargain with the stallholders. He's a good shopper, going not for flash looks or the most expensive option but instead for the solidly built and utilitarian.

Loading up a tuk-tuk we take the goods to his room, which he now shares with his younger sister, Bounlee, who is due to start her two year course of training as a kindergarten teacher next month and whose college fees we have offered to pay.

I know you've been dying to ask, so I'll put you out of your misery and tell you: for you to buy a cup of coffee every alternate day over the course of a year, in any major western city, would cost roughly the same as we pay for Chanthy and Bounlee to attend college for that year, plus pay the annual rent on their room. Which puts things in some proportion.

The concrete walls of their room were once

white. But they are now a grubby non-colour. We suggest to Chanthy that if he gets permission from his landlord, we could paint the walls. He likes that idea a lot and assures us that it won't be necessary to get any permissions if we buy the paint ourselves. So they can be put up again later we carefully peel back the corners of handwritten aphorisms in English that Chanthy has stuck up exhorting himself to *Keep Doing...Follow Your Dream*. Telling himself that *Education Is The Key of Life*, and *Even The Life Is Difficult Now...But It Becomes Better In The Future If You Don't Give Up*.

Back at Luang Prabang's equivalent of Bunnings Hardware warehouse, where we had first met Dao Midgley almost a year ago, we buy large cans of white paint and the best brushes available. These are very poor quality and from my all too vast experience as an interior and exterior housepainter I fear they will shed hairs like crazy.

Buying paint

Bounlee holds the ladder while brother, Chanthy paints their room

Very early next morning, in a vain attempt to avoid the heat, those fears are confirmed. But by eleven o'clock Iain, wearing just his underpants and a T-shirt and in a perpetual lather of sweat, along with Chanthy, have painted the four walls. While Bounlee and I have made ourselves as useful as possible by continually moving their meagre possessions around to make room for the borrowed ladder.

I needed to go to the loo but wished I hadn't. Chanthy apologizes for the primitive conditions and then asks if I would also like to see their 'bathing place'. While we walk up the incline, in front of the row of other identical rooms, I work out how much the owner of this set-up makes from his overall rentals. A good investment when you consider how little he offers.

Cleaning brushes in Chanthy's 'Bathroom'

Two old enamel baths are propped up on bricks on a small concrete slab by the side of the track leading up by the side of the building. The showerhead is tied on to a rusted pipe.

There is no privacy at all. As we approach, a couple of people wait patiently for their turn to stand in the bath. The young woman already bathing does so while wearing a modest sarong. The soapy water from her ablutions simply runs out the empty plughole and wends its way down a track it has worn for itself in front of the row of rooms.

Chanthy says he and his sister will give the room a second coat of paint tomorrow on their own and Iain gratefully accedes. We all stand around admiring the cleansing effect the paint has had. The woman who runs a noodle stall behind the rooms and who has been watching the work going on now brings us a bowl each of noodles and smilingly refuses payment.

Over the next few days there is a flurry of emails back and forth between us and our daughter who tells us that she and her now fiancé Jay have booked flights to visit Australia for Christmas and New Year and they would like us all to camp our way the 800 kilometres down along the coast from our place in the New South Wales Northern Rivers area to Sydney. This is something of a challenge because that's the very height of the Australian holiday season when every man and his dog takes to the road. And lining it all up remotely from Laos is a serious added complication

Emails are not sufficient. Booking camping sites for this time of the year needs charmingly persuasive voice contact and even that is no guarantee. It takes concentrated time but Iain pulls it all together.

We visit Florent Lavabre again at his RMA office where he introduces us to Ai Vong Cha Leong, the director of a construction company who says he could provide machinery and material for the road, when we get the funds. Good contact to know. It is all about putting it out there.

We also visit Kopnoi, the handicraft shop, so Chanthy can introduce us to his employer Celine, show us around and listen to his sales pitch, which is very impressive. His English language skills are so improved, along with his self-confidence.

Now its time for another visit to the morning market for some buffalo blood sausages that Chanthy assures us are his Mum's favourite; no doubt because of their high iron content that her hard-worked body must crave. Then a three-hour glide down the flooded Mekong, followed by a bone-jarring tok-tok ride into NaLin village,

One day, we promise ourselves, we will take a boat all the way down the Mekong from Luang Prabang to Vientiane, a two or three day journey at least. Just some books, the crew and us. But this time its another 'working trip' and we have to be satisfied with landing not at the village of Hadsaikham, as we did the first time, because the flood season's fast, full, swirling waters make that too dangerous. Instead we pull in a few kilometers further downstream and scramble up through treacherous sucking mud into Khoktum.

Chanthy's Dad, Thongkhan, is there to meet us

and again it's like coming home. We pile the food, bottled water and ourselves into the tray of the tok-tok and try to wedge ourselves in among the goods to make the best of what we know is going to be a tough journey, but worth it, because at the end Buachanh, Chanthy's mother, is there to greet us with a welcoming smile.

If anything the stark poverty of life in NaLin strikes us with even more force. We join in the village daily rituals, including the evening bathe in the river that demands steady legs in the increased current. Before the others return from the fields, Chanthy tells us he has something he wants to show us. From his expression it is obvious this is something important to him and that he is a little anxious about how we will react. But we encourage him and from the upper floor where his parents sleep on roll out mats he brings down a maquette, a small wooden model of a two-story home. 'I make this,' he tells us shyly and when we congratulate him on his skills he explains; 'This is the house I want to build in Luang Prabang, when I finish college and have a good job, a wife and two children. This my dream'.

'Step by step,' we smile encouragingly. He nods in agreement.

We have noticed that since our first visit a small space has been curtained off at the end of the main room nearest to the doorway. 'My cousin, Mr. Pho Simaneevong is living here now,' Chanthy tells us and goes on to elaborate, 'he is actually the younger brother of my mother's mother.' In our language, a great uncle.

Seventy-eight year old Mr. Pho has been married since he was a very young man. He is still married and his equally elderly wife now lives with members of her own extended family in a village close to Vientiane. 'They were unable to have children', Chanthy explains, 'so they have no one to look after them and as they can no longer look after each other, he has come to live with us.' This is a statement, without any underlying comment and certainly no rancour. It is just a matter of fact.

Mr. Pho's 'home' is now a 2 metres by 3 metres space curtained off from the main room of the Sisombuth home. 'My Mother takes care of him. It is difficult sometimes because my Mother and Father have to go to the fields very early every morning and they must leave him here, but my Mother comes back in the middle of the day to check he is ok.'

My heart goes out to this 78 -year -old man bereft of his wife of almost sixty years; more so I guess because he is only a year older than Iain and also because Iain and I have been together for almost fifty years. So I know that the feelings of loss must be excruciating. I ask Chanthy if Mr. Pho and his wife maintain contact. 'They speak on the phone once a week,' he says. Mr. Pho has no specific illness. He is simply old. Later that day he asks us, through Chanthy, if we have any medicine, 'To make me feel younger.'

Almost toothless and all but deaf, he eats very little of the meals prepared for him and finds it hard to follow the numerous conversations of people who come and go from the house in a constantly changing flow. In a country where the average life expectancy when Mr. Pho was born was considerable lower than it is for a Lao born in 2012 when it was registered as 60 for men and 64 for women 78 is indeed very old. The man's body is little more than fine, weathered skin stretched over bones. But he can bend his knees and squat comfortably on the ground far more easily than Iain and I.

Fisherman Pho Simaneevong makes a new net

Some days he spends most of the time on his mattress hung about with mosquito nets. Other days he sits cross-legged for hours, in the light that comes in through the doorway. With thick-lensed spectacles perched on the end of his nose he patiently knots fine nylon into the complex weave of a fishing net. 'Before he became old,' Chanthy explains, 'he was a very good, strong fisherman in the Mekong.' I let my mind roam across the huge social changes Mr. Pho must have witnessed. 'Please tell him about The Road,' I ask Chanthy. The old man's face lights up and he places a hand on his heart to sign thank you.

The villagers assemble and we are again welcomed with a traditional basi, followed by the evening meal, all of which takes place on the hard floor. After the ceremony the women collect up the pots and plates and take them to the tiny dark space, off the back of the room, that passes for a kitchen while the men hunker down on the mats to watch Iain's two short Road to NaLin videos.

Villagers watch our short videos

There is the silence of concentration as the pictures flicker and the music emanates from Iain's Mac. I find it impossible to imagine what emotions those men are experiencing as they see shots of Iain and me on the beach at Bondi asking for help to build The Road to NaLin.

Their lives revolve around the seasons, the planting and harvesting of the rice in their family lots, now with the very recent addition of hops grown for the Lao brewery that produces the popular Beer Lao. For those lucky enough to have pigs or chickens there needs to be animal feed. What matters to them is how long the dry season lasts, the coming of the rains, what damage the inevitable storms wreak, the level the annual floodwaters reach; the inevitable cycle of marriages, births, deaths. Most of them have made the arduous tok-tok and rickety taxi-truck journey to Luang Prabang. But the ongoing constant daily demands of their plots limit their usual horizons to the District capital of Muang Nan, fifteen kilometers away and then only when a medical emergency necessitates a visit to a primitive clinic, or to barter their produce for farming implements or additional foodstuffs. Bondi Beach is surely a mirage: more ludicrously unbelievable even than the existence of giant neighbour Thailand across the Mekong River.

We wake with the pre-dawn crowing of the cockerels and hear muffled voices at the open doorway. Chanthy who is already up and helping prepare breakfast comes across to our malarial protection mosquito net. Thank you Bill and Melinda Gates, what enormous good your monies are doing.

'Suspicion man is come', Chanthy informs us.

Suspicion man turns out to be 'superstition'

man, Thongdy Thongsamou, the former Buddhist monk who always officiates at all basi and other celebrations in the village. We squat beside Thongdy on the floor and he ties a string, bearing a small metal bead, around our necks while murmuring incantations and stroking our skin. Quite spooky.

'He wishes you good times for the future,' Chanthy says and as we nod appreciatively, 'Very lucky for you. You should give him five thousand kip.' Eighty cents.

This time, as we leave, a large contingent of men from the village comes to wave us off on the boat that will carry us back up the Mekong. Among them is the principal of the small school for whom we had again brought books published by Big Brother Mouse. Before we leave he tells us what his students would really like to have is another football, as the one we had given them on our previous visit has been kicked to bursting. They would also appreciate a set of metal boules for the students to play petanque. We assure him that we will get these things down to him asap.

On the boat Chanthy is unusually quiet, pensive and I ask him if he is feeling okay. He nods before saying quietly, 'I cannot be a farmer. I am not strong like my brother Jai.' We both look down at his slight frame. 'But it is also because I do not want to live in poor village. I love my parents but I do not want to live like they have done.' In a show of understanding I put my hand on his. Laos can be difficult sometimes for a committed serial hugger like me.

Non-hugging happens again when, back in Luang Prabang, we meet up once again with our novice friend, Khamchanh. Iain and he shake hands warmly but I force myself to stand back at a distance and make a nop. Khamchanh smiles, 'How you going mate?' he says in a good imitation of a broad Australian accent and we all laugh.

We talk about his family where everything seems to be going well and his studies, which he obviously enjoys enormously. 'But,' he pauses, 'I am thinking of leaving the wat.' When we express surprise and ask what he plans to do he tells us, 'I am thinking of studying computer design, perhaps at the American College in Vientiane and perhaps,' his smile broadens, 'perhaps in Bangkok!' He shakes his head as if in disbelief himself. 'It depends on the grades I get for my final year at the monk's high school.' He is excited at the prospect and we discuss what is involved and offer any help.

Khamchanh wants to talk about the books he has been reading and of course football. As the sunlight fades, the colour of his orange robes blends into the colour of the wall decoration of the main wat hall, so that Khamchanh appears to become a part of the building. I am anxious how it will be for him in the outside world.

Over the next couple of days we stock up on small handicrafts to take home as gifts and take a tuk-tuk a little way out of town to visit Dao Midgley who has invited us to visit her home. The view of the range of mountains from the windows of the big airy main room is spectacular. Dao is in her element; she is like a butterfly freshly released from its chrysalis, totally at ease with herself...at home.

She takes us on a visit to the village and the school on the slopes behind her house that she and Stephen have helped to build and where I meet several families of Hmong people. Dao introduces me to a woman who is embroidering atop the intricate appliqué design she has created for a large wall hanging.

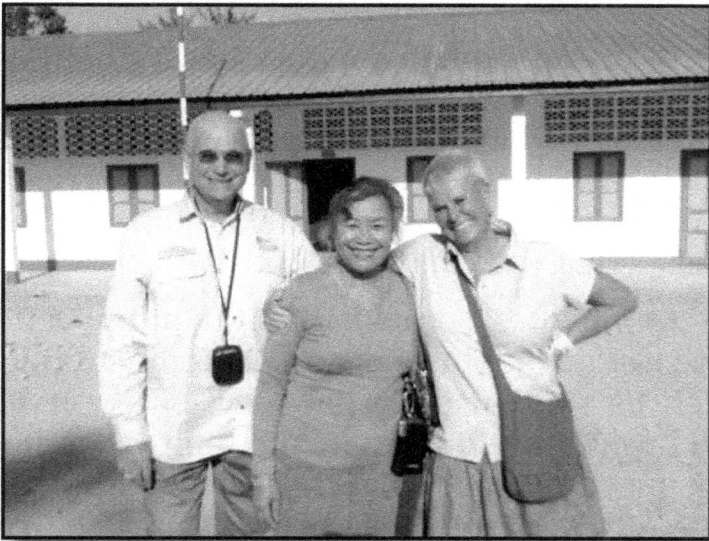

Stephen and Dao Midgley and the newest of three schools they have built near Luang Prabang

Back at her own house, Dao shows us some of the other handicrafts these women have made and that she will take back to Australia to sell at the fund-raising events she holds in her own home.

We can hardly guess how successful this

concept will later prove to be for us back in Australia, in raising funds for an extended road project, of which more later

We discuss further ideas in which to use these women's arts that of course must not be allowed to die in the face of factory mass production. But before we leave, Dao again stresses the need for us to obtain the all-important letter of agreement from the villagers of NaLin. 'Don't forget,' she wags her forefinger, 'most important, red chops. The more the merrier.'

When we explain what we need, Chanthy with his usual quick intelligence, immediately understands what we want and more importantly, why. He promises to get the letter, no worries about the chops and we say, 'this is our address in Australia that you can post it to.'

At the post office, that Chanthy has never before visited but knew of as a government building, though he was unsure what function it served, we buy a brown envelope, write our address on it, put a blank piece of paper in it as a substitute for the village letter, have it weighed and buy the correct amount of postal stamps to send it by airmail to Australia.

Chanthy clutches the envelope to him as if it were a life raft and it suddenly dawns on me what he is pondering. 'It goes along with a lot of other envelopes and parcels,' I tell him, 'in a plane.' He gives a relieved smile and I feel a little surge of almost envy for all the wonders of the world we take so for granted and he has yet to discover.

But we will not be home in Australia for several weeks. We are heading off to Shanghai to do some more research into our plans for having my 70th birthday party there in one year's time. Checking on accommodation, and arrangements at the Peace Hotel for the birthday dinner. Equally importantly, we are going to try to arrange a permit to enter Tibet and to make the two-day and two-night train journey from Shanghai to Lhasa.

13

A DIRECT APPEAL

We hadn't mentioned to anyone before we left home that in addition to going to Laos we were hoping to also visit Tibet. We knew that the vagaries of visas and the required special permits meant it is impossible to be certain you will get to Tibet, until you are actually there. But happily, get there we did!

Back home in Australia, after visiting not only Tibet but also the extraordinarily interesting panda breeding sanctuary in Chengdu, we find the letter from the villagers of NaLin and signed by the headman, Mr. Dith has arrived. Adorned with several red chops, stamps that include a hammer and sickle in their design, it is waiting for us at our local post

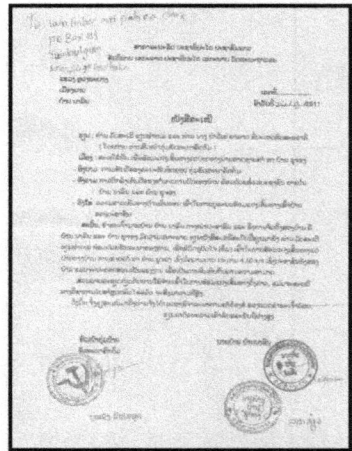

The village letter

office/general store like a welcome-home gift. At the time we had no idea how helpful it would be in the future.

Also in the envelope is a letter from Chanthy painstakingly carefully handwritten on that squared paper Europeans use in which each letter sits neatly inside its own printed box. In it he thanks us again for every small thing we have done over the past year and concludes by saying how much his life has changed for the better.

We design and produce our hard copy round up of the year's happenings as an illustrated card that we send out annually. This of course includes the first news many of our friends have had of The Road to NaLin project. Australia then closes up shop and settles down to enjoy the summer.

End of year festivities, including a camping trip down along the beautiful north coast of New South Wales with our daughter and her now-fiancé, take over our lives. In Sydney Jay is introduced and welcomed by family and friends. There is an engagement luncheon and the city turns on its powerfully seductive headlights of dazzling amazements; fireworks, coastal walks, open air dining, Harbour restaurants and so on; not to mention the sparkling ocean, faultless surf breaks, street markets, open air cinema and the Opera House. Even the big blue grouper comes out to give us the eye as we do our daily swims off Clovelly. It is all such perfection, as if specially produced by the NSW Department of Tourism, that I feel driven to tell Jay, 'its not always like this you know,' in case later he feels he has been conned.

We decide its time to put out a definite appeal for donations to The Road project. Although there's no specific request for contributions in it, friends and others have had time to read our round up of Season's Greetings news and have an inkling of what we're becoming involved in. So we also decide that although it will cost money, a hard copy direct appeal is more likely to grab their attention than yet another email.

We design and have printed a couple of different versions of this appeal, with the additional modern twist of the URL for the Road to NaLin website Iain has put together. The website contains some fairly stark images of the village and the shocking road. One version of the appeal goes to friends the other to people we know less well. All these are mailed out.

It's a year plus a bit since we started on this journey and I notice changes that have occurred in myself. Perhaps the biggest is that I have become somewhat barefaced about asking for donations, though only because it is not for myself.

Fortunately, because none of us know what the future holds, I have no idea that the oncoming year will be a one of whack-you-in-your-face experiences both of intense happiness and of equally overwhelming sadness;

The appeal for funds also contains a Facebook address. We have earnest discussions about this; seeing Facebook as being potentially very invasive while on the other hand a great way to spread the word about our project.

Even this tentative step into what, with Luddite antipathy I view as a murky world, brings instant demands for learning new skills, at least for me. Within less than a week of our mail out our Facebook page lights up with comments and 'like' ticks all of which we feel honour-bound to respond to personally. I console myself that this time-consuming process will bring in the required monies.

Out there in the other world, even the most casual inquiry from anybody who asks us more or less in passing, 'G'day, haven't seen you for a while, how you going?' is met with our by now polished responses about The Road to NaLin project. We have even taken to carrying copies of our appeal letters in our car so we can produce them on these occasions. We have also been known to leave them on the doorsteps of anyone who expresses even the slightest degree of polite interest. At least we realize we have become obsessed.

The monetary rejoinder to our appeal is immensely gratifying, though not really overwhelming. Donations begin to arrive in the form of cash, personal checks, direct to the RNL fund bank account and as well through PayPal and MasterCard. These last two forms of payment had taken Iain a great deal of time and patience to establish. Monies come from unexpected rather than anticipated sources. Phil's Bathols' original positive statement that we surely know sixty people who will give $1000 is quickly put to rout.

The donations I most appreciate are the unsolicited ones. A woman swims up to us in our ocean creek one day and pushes $50 into the top of my bathers. 'For your road.' Just as well Australian money is waterproof.

Iain magically adds a graphic financial thermometer to the RNL website he has created that illustrates the slow growth of the fund. He also creates a running blog he regularly updates. All donations are banked and precise records kept. We are far, far more careful with all of this than we have ever been with our own monies.

In one of our seemingly non-stop Road conversations Iain comes up with the idea of Donation Certificates. 'People like recognition,' he says. It is also that he likes to design.

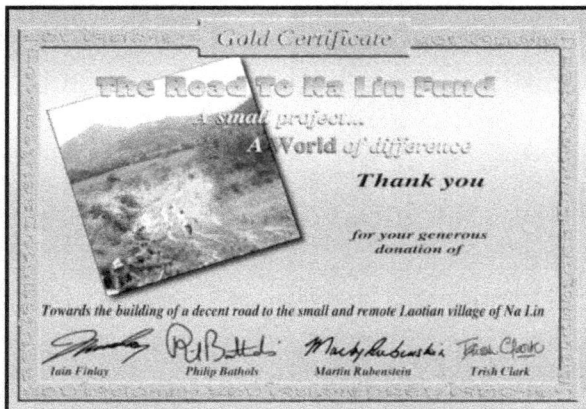

NaLin Gold Certificate

The resultant certificates, Bronze, Silver, Gold, and Platinum, apart from giving recognition are decorated all around   the edge with the words, thank you very much, *kopchai lai lai*, written over and over in the beautiful Lao script. 'I'll do a Diamond one, for $5,000 and over,' Iain says, 'you never know.'

This positive attitude is just one of the reasons why I love him but to be honest both of us feel rather deflated by the low level response. It may be judgmental, but I don't mind saying I felt a number of people we thought we knew, could do with some rearrangement to their priorities. Especially those who if for no other reason than at their age, they are, like us, playing in their quickly shortening terminal innings. I become aware of looking at life and people differently.

At a funeral, in the Blue Mountains, west of Sydney, of a close and dear friend, the world-renowned mountain-climber Lincoln Hall, who died after an awful, yearlong battle with mesothelioma, we meet Dick and Pip Smith.

Dick, the extremely successful business entrepreneur, had given enormous support to Lincoln and his ventures over the decades. When Pip speaks to me she comments on our Christmas card and the follow up appeal for RNL donations. She asks sensible, penetrating questions about The Road, about how we became involved and what impact The Road will have. I find myself relieved from my grief over Lincoln to be talking about Chanthy, explaining his background and his dreams for his future as well as about the village and villagers of NaLin. I feel she is really listening, not just being polite. Like any family, the Smiths and their two daughters have been through a bit. Despite their great financial success they have remained grounded. It is impossible not to feel that this is due in very large part to Pip's strength of character.

We drive northward home and within a week I have a panic attack, my heart rate goes off the scale, I spend a scary night in hospital and the very empathetic doctor releases me on condition that I promise to take medication; which I do, for a month.

Back home Iain firmly suggests that I do not read the emails about Lincoln that have flooded in but that instead I take time out to knit. I have plans for making a king-sized throw as a wedding gift for our daughter. It will be knitted in squares, each with a different design, the whole sewn together and backed with silk held in place with pearl buttons. It will be edged with a knitted border. All of it, the woolen yarn, silk backing and buttons are cream coloured because Zara, unlike her mother, is not into bright. She goes more for the elegant, classy look.

Knitting has always soothed my spirit. While I sit in the autumnal light and knit, Iain soldiers on. In the quest to find backing for a road engineer he re-contacts Engineers Without Borders and SMEC, the Snowy Mountains Engineering Corporation both of whom have been let slip, as a result of all that's been happening. He also gets on the Net and tracks down Australian companies working in Laos in the hope that one of them will see the public relations benefit of investing in The Road.

Though we don't verbally admit as much to each other, we both know the other one is feeling a bit low in spirits, anxious we have bitten off rather more than we can chew.

What's that they say about the darkest hour comes before the dawn?

14

THREE DOLLARS and FIVE THOUSAND!

Six-year-old Zoe Griffis of Noosa, in Queensland, has saved up $3 from her pocket money and gives it to us, all in small change, when we attend the Opening of her father Anthony's art exhibition. We have known Anthony and his wife, Paula Bycroft, since back in the days when we were with the Beyond 2000 program and the two of them still work there as producers, writers and presenters; though Anthony is taking a year away from the TV mêlée to establish himself as a water colour painter.

6-year old Zoe Griffis

'This is for The Road,' Zoe tells us. We hug her and thank her very much, telling her what a special gift it is and how much difference it will make in Laos. This is true. $3 is more than Chanthy earns for a day spent in the Luang Prabang craft shop where he works and more than his parents can make from their literally back-breaking seven days a week ten hour days in their rice paddy.

Before beginning the drive up to Brisbane to Anthony's exhibition we had gone into our own local village where Iain had emptied our Post Office box of the usual assortment of unappealing window envelopes. Not until we are out on the highway does he begin to sort through them and coming across one with a return address in Terry Hills lets out a low groan assuming it was from an oddball political lobbyist who latched on to us during our time in public life and from whom we have been attempting, with varying degrees of success over some years, to release ourselves. 'Don't bother opening it,' I say, 'Just tear it up'.

But Iain, with his kinder spirit, slits it open and lets out a joyful whoop. '$5000 from Pip and Dick Smith!' he shouts and we both burst into mad peals of laughter. 'Just as well I didn't tear it .'

So, irrationally, we feel we have turned a corner or come out of a tunnel or, anyway that things are looking up. This is the somewhat exhausting roller-coaster ride we have come to anticipate.

That very evening we email our thanks to the Smiths and the very next day we post out Donation Certificates to Zoe and to Pip and Dick.

$5000 from Dick and Pip Smith

Within the week The Road fund receives another boost: a generous cheque from writer Bryce Courtenay. Iain has known Bryce for almost sixty years. They met in what was then known as Northern Rhodesia, working on the copper belt; young men dreaming of their whole lives ahead of them and what full lives they have been. We already knew that Bryce had been diagnosed with stomach cancer, but in the phone conversation to thank him Bryce was upbeat, while at the same time frankly accepting of what the diagnosis meant.

This lift to our spirits helps us over the news that the Engineers Without Borders group, after further chasing, informs us that they can't help and similarly, SMEC, again after further chasing, fobs us off once more with vague promises of getting back in touch, which they never keep.

Undeterred, Iain decides it is an opportune time to again approach our local Rotary Club. We have printed a hard copy of the information on the RNL website. There are two reasons why I feel this is the way to go; firstly if I were going to give sizeable support, which is what we want from Rotary, I would want to know the sort of detail this backgrounder includes; such as in-depth information about Laos, its history, geography, society, economics, politics and so forth. But also, not everyone is enamoured of websites, in fact many are unable to use them. Whereas having a hard copy in their hands, being able to turn the pages, see the maps and photographs, gives tangible proof-positive something is really happening. It is also something easily passed on to others with no need to explain websites, codes and so forth. As it turns out, my assessment is accurate and it seemed at one point as though it would pay off, in spades. Though of course we have no way of knowing this when we drop the bound copy, that also held a our six minute DVD, in to the mechanical workshop, whose owner/operator, Ian Simpson, is the Secretary of the Club. It is just another pebble thrown into the pool.

Then one morning, among the emails I am still not reading, Iain opens one from Graham Read whose name was given to us by SMEC in Melbourne as manager of their office in Vientiane. He thinks he may be able to help with The Road and he would like us to phone him. Laos is four hours behind us. It's a nerve-wracking four-hour wait. But well worth the angst because Graham knows all about roads like the one we are planning; what is necessary and what is involved. He's lived and worked as an engineer in south east Asia for a long time. All this gives him a handle on our motivation. There's no need for long-winded, all-encompassing explanations. It is so freeing to be able to converse in mutually understandable shorthand. We arrange to send him the RNL website address and our DVD and after the conversation finishes we both feel very positive about possible outcomes

Aaah but there is, as they say, many a slip twixt cup and lip.

Around this time at a RNL Committee Meeting, which is a dinner at our place, Phil Bathols brings up an idea he had mooted right from the start of the project: a fund raising concert, or concerts, plural. We say this sounds like an extra good idea, because it should help to raise the profile of the project by giving us a hook on which to hang a story we hope will attract that all important aspect of fund raising: media coverage.

Phil offers a percentage of the profits from a series of concerts he is planning to celebrate the fiftieth anniversary of Bob Dylan as a recording artist. We happily accept his generosity.

Dylan seems like a good fit even though right from the start we know Bob Dylan is not for everyone. In recent years he hasn't helped his own cause. Perhaps he never has. Maybe he's never wanted to. He came along before packaged talent was the be all and end all. But now we feel Bob Dylan's name and the ideals he represents could at least perhaps help us build the Road to Na Lin.

Phil elaborates on his project. He is putting together a five-some of popular local talent. The idea is to celebrate not only the 50th anniversary of Bob Dylan's career as a recording artist but also to honour his remarkable legacy of forty-seven albums and more than five hundred songs. 'We want everybody, performers and audience, to have a great time,' Phil says, ' and if we can also make some money for The Road, that's even better.'

The concerts are planned, one day after another, for three days in early July 2012, at the Palais Theatre in Melbourne, the Lyric Theatre, QPAC in Brisbane and the Opera House in Sydney. Rehearsals will take place in the afternoons before the performances.

Kav Temperley of *Eskimo Joe* at the Bob Dylan
Night concert in Sydney at the Opera House

It is a substantial production to put up and then hold in place: to create an appealing performance balance from the diverse talents of people who have never before worked together, as well as the logistical demands of travel, not only for the singers but for the band, plus their instruments, along with a mass of sound equipment is a big ask. But after all this is show business.

We decide to set up a *Road To Na Lin* stall in the lobby of each of the three venues in turn, showcasing via our video on a loop, the needs of NaLin village and the horrible condition of the road we want to fix.

All three of the concerts, we thought, were sensational. But despite all of the effort and financial risk on Phil's part, something doesn't quite gel and the financial numbers don't live up to expectations so in the end not only do the concerts fail to make a profit they don't reach break even figures. Nor do our stalls in the theatre lobbies produce any donations. So our expectations of a reasonable windfall for The Road from the three events falls flat and we personally are out of pocket by quite an amount for our airfares and accommodation.

A short while later, Laos jumps into the news again and once more for the wrong reasons, even if most Australians are a little unsure of exactly where Laos is. A distressing number of Aussie lads and young men from other western countries are having serious accidents and some have died in tubing incidents on the river at Vang Vieng.

Young travelers and backpackers have suddenly discovered this village, more or less halfway between Vientiane and Luang Prabang and set against an improbably beautiful backdrop of mountains. What had been for decades a method used by farmers to transport their crops to market, by floating them downriver on rafts created from inflated large inner tubes becomes a thrilling ride in an exotic location for youngsters pushing the limits. Bars and hostels quickly spring up to cater for this new scene and inevitably alcohol and other drugs follow. The deaths make the style of headlines the media thrives on. Suddenly Lao is 'hot'.

But not, it seems, for our fund-raising efforts.

Then, one morning, while having a self-serving wallow in this trough of despair, the phone rings and a man's voice announces himself to be Mr. Bee.

'Yes. Right...Mr. Bee', I repeat skeptically.

'John Bee, I'm with Broadbeach Rotary and I'm interested in your Road to NaLin project. Could we meet?'

15

ROTARY AGAIN

During the following week we make the forty-minute drive up to another world known as the Gold Coast. The Bee family home has a plethora of rooms, white leather sofas, and a swimming pool. In their garden there's a huge and beautiful macadamia tree, shading a mound of toe-tickling thick lawn above one of the canals for which this part of the Australian coast is famous. Beside this is the Bee's private jetty at which their boat is moored.

But the first thing we notice is the print edition of our Laos Backgrounder lying in its bright coloured ring binder on the big glass-topped coffee table. John explains: 'At our annual convention, a couple of weeks ago, the President of the Murwillumbah branch came up to me and said, 'I hear you are interested in Laos. Well then you might want to take a look at this,' and handed it to me. It was the copy we had left at Ian Simpson's workshop. How fortuitous that we had approached our local

Rotary again. Another ripple in the pond or so we think at the time.

John's wife Marilyn is off at work, running her financial planners office, but John has shopped at the patisserie across the road and produces a gateau and tea. We sit with their dog Buddy, a plump poodle-cross, under the macadamia tree and talk about Laos.

Once again, to our relief, it turns out we can talk in shorthand because John and Marilyn and their two sons lived in Laos for eight years in the seventies and eighties. John, who is now retired from fulltime work, was employed by the World Bank as an agronomist and in this role spent time in many and varied areas of the country, so we're off to a good start. We don't need to explain about the condition of the roads and more importantly what a quantum beneficial difference a good road makes to any small village there. He has also read our backgrounder.

John is quite frank with us about the Broadbeach branch of Rotary he and Marilyn have joined. 'We did our research and looked around in the area for a Club with a somewhat younger and more diverse membership.'

We take this explanation as polite code for assuring us the Broadbeach membership is not made up of elderly retired white males. In mutual response to this candid approach we tell John we view the possibility of being taken on as one of their projects by Rotary as something akin to receiving a Papal Blessing.

John further explains that being newly accepted members, he and Marilyn need to tread lightly and not appear to be attempting to bulldoze members into action. But, having said that, because of course that is exactly what they *are* doing, they are very keen to organize a visit by a dozen or so Broadbeach Rotarians to Laos towards the end of the year and he says, 'We're thinking it would be great if we could take them to your village.' Our hearts leap.

The couple is planning to have a social get together in a couple of weeks for all members of their Club who may be interested in visiting Laos. They plan to show two videos about Laos and the legacy of the so-called Secret War that occurred there during the sixties and early seventies. We boldly invite ourselves along, offering to show our own ten-minute DVD and give a brief chat. We sense John is a little hesitant.

Iain assures him, 'I'll be very low-key.' 'And I won't talk at all,' I promise rashly. That seems to settle John's anxieties.

In addition to the Bees and us there are fifteen people at the function when it is held a fortnight later. A couple of the Club members are women.

After everybody has eaten from the array of snacks provided, the Bees get down to the nitty-gritty and announce a showing of *The Most Secret Place on Earth*. This is the documentary film I mentioned previously when it was screened on national television. It is about the highly illegal, secret operation waged by the CIA throughout the sixties and seventies against the Vietcong and North Vietnamese troops coming down through a supposedly neutral Laos along the Ho Chi Minh Trail and into South Vietnam.

Its not a pretty travelogue picture, but one that lays bare the sad truth that Laos, during this period, as explained before, became the most heavily bombed place on earth, with some two million tonnes of ordnance, including napalm and cluster bombs, dropped over vast areas of eastern and central Laos. The other possibly even more tragic statistic is that 30% of the bombs dropped did not explode and have left fully one third of the country contaminated. Every year, even now, these UXO cause 100 new casualties. 60% of these result in death and 40% are children.

The second award-winning documentary the Bees put up on their extra-large screen television set was *Bomb Harvest* in which laconic Australian bomb-disposal expert Laith Stevens is shown working in different parts of Laos, helping to train locals in the extremely dangerous work of dismantling UXO, or unexploded ordnance, left over from the American bombings.

Then it's Iain's turn to show our ten-minute piece, to talk about The Road and to answer any questions all of which he does in an appealingly low-key and accessible manner. There's not a great deal of lightness in any of the three films, but in the end we got the feeling the club members empathize with the villagers' plight.

More tea and coffee is followed by open questions to Marilyn about what travelers to Laos can expect. It is far from certain that John and Marilyn can get up the numbers to make a visit to Laos financially viable. It is at the end of this meeting that members will be required to make a definite decision about whether or not they are committed to going. They will need to put their money where their mouths are shortly thereafter. It is important, as John and Marilyn have told us, the journey is sold to them as an adventure but also they know what they are up for, financially and in other ways. I try not to hear Iain's polite response to the woman who asks if her expensive sneakers are likely to be ruined by the mud on The Road.

We leave feeling satisfied we have made a positive appeal for possible participation by the Broadbeach Rotary Club in the RNL project. If only we'd had our future glasses on!

16

AN ENGINEER and ANOTHER $5000!

Around this time Iain decides to chase up Graham Read in Vientiane who, since promising to get back to us shortly, has gone silent. The reason, Iain discovers, is that there has been a corporate shake-up: SMEC'S office in Vientiane has been closed and Graham has been posted to their office in Hong Kong. Undeterred, Iain phones him there. Graham is full of apologies and gives him the name and contact details of another engineer, James Grindey, who is working for an engineering firm in Vientiane. He also promises he will phone James himself, right now.

Just to make doubly sure we decide to immediately email our background information package to James Grindey ourselves.

We visit the office of a now somewhat disconsolate concert promoter Phil Bathols, still in the doldrums over the Bob Dylan Nights tour. Iain rattles on about the highs and lows of being self-employed, something about which we know all too well and in an aside, to hopefully take Phil's mind off his business woes, he asks him, 'What's with all the boxes?' indicating the cartons stacked against one wall that are squeezing Phil into one side of his room.

'Books,' Phil says morosely. '*Up Till Now*, the biography of William Shatner, he explains further. When we brought him out last year my business partner had a brainstorm and decided that we could sell his biography at his show. I can't recall how many we bought, but anyway those are the ones left over.'

'How many are there?'

'I don't know; five hundred, maybe a thousand'

'What will you do with them?' I ask.

'Take them to the tip I suppose, though even that will cost money. I have to get rid of them, they're a constant reminder of failure: not a failure of the tour, that was a great success. It is just that we didn't sell the books '

'We'll take some,' Iain says brightly. I groan inwardly.

'We'll sell them and put the money towards The Road.' My heart sinks as I imagine now having to set up a roadside bookstall.

'That's fine by me,' Phil shrugs his shoulders, 'take as many as you like.'

We carry six cartons down to my little car.

'Whom will we sell them to?' I manage to ask as we drive home.

'Trekkies of course.' Iain sounds amazed I even need to inquire.

'Remember all those people wearing Star Trek gear at the show?'

We had attended William Shatner's extremely enjoyable show and been blown away by the large section of the audience who had come dressed up as Captain Kirk, Shatner's pivotal role in *Star Trek* as commander of the Starship Enterprise, as well as other members of the crew.

'But we don't know any Trekkies,' I say.

As it turned out, much to our amazement, we do. We just didn't know they were Trekkies. They had kept their fandom quietly to themselves I guess. But once we starting asking around they kept coming out of the woodwork and buying the books. One friend even took a box-load to sell at a street market in Sydney's inner suburb of Newtown.

'They'll be on the Net,' Iain was certain.

Of course he was correct. There was one big club in our same zone and yes; they would take a hundred copies for an upcoming Science Fact and Fiction Conference. All we had to do was beam them up Scotty, perhaps at warp speed, to Brisbane. This Road to NaLin effort was certainly widening our more usual horizons.

In an email John and Marilyn Bee declare they

have managed to bring enough Rotarians on board to make their trip to Laos feasible. And importantly, they would like to visit NaLin village. They would like to look at it as a possibility for future involvement by their Club, John says. They would also like to talk further to us about contacts in the village, in Luang Prabang and in Vientiane. We can feel Rotary inching closer to embracing us.

A day later there's an email from James Grindey in Vientiane. James, a senior executive in the Lao engineering company, the Lao Consulting Group, is offering, free of charge, the professional services of one of the company's Senior Road Engineers. Graham Reid in Hong Kong, as I've just mentioned, has alerted James, to our needs and James explains that, if we agree to pick up the per diems and travel expenses of their engineer, the company will pay his fees. Could we phone to discuss all this?

There is still enough of the working day left in Vientiane in which to call James in his office. Despite, as we learn later, having lived in Laos for thirty years, James has retained a distinct and comforting Manchester accent. He has a warm, friendly manner and is also very professional in his questions about The Road. He has read through the background information package we had emailed through, so he knows sufficient for this stage of the game. Apart from thanking him for his generous offer of a Senior Roads Engineer, we arrange to let him know as soon as possible what our timings are for our next visit to Vientiane.

Feeling now that nothing can slow our progress, we spend most of the next day attempting to email and then fax the forms we have filled in to apply to the Australian Government's Direct Aid Program for assistance with building The Road. These are monies given at the discretion of individual Australian Ambassadors in a number of countries that would benefit from even such small-scale aid. We add a personal letter to the Ambassador requesting a brief meeting with her to discuss our RNL project.

We then go for our daily ocean creek swim and when we return there is polite message in a soft voice on our answering machine from a secretarial assistant at the Australian Embassy in Laos informing us that our email has been received, faxes, ditto, and that there will be an official response shortly.

Within twenty-four hours there is a personal email from Lynda Worthaisong, the Australian Ambassador to Laos. It is positive and pleasingly informal. She suggests we let her know exactly when we will be in Vientiane so we can lock in a time for a meeting. She looks forward to that.

Fortunately an actual physical invitation to our daughter's wedding in San Francisco has recently arrived so what had been up to then a somewhat loose arrangement has at last been firmed up. We discuss timings and decide to give ourselves ten days to enjoy this family occasion. Working forward from that we settle on a date that will allow us two days to travel back halfway across the globe from San Francisco to Laos and we email that date to Ms. Worthaisong. We also warn her that there is a hard copy of our application winging its way toward her. The appointment is made.

We let James Grindey know we are meeting with the Ambassador and we arrange to meet him later on that same day.

This means there is now a framework within which we have to make the rest of our plans for the year fit.

A couple in their seventies, whom we have known both separately for more than forty years and as an item for twenty, decide to get legally married. The wedding is in Sydney.

Happily the celebrant for the wedding, Christine Howard, is a wonderful woman, also a good friend and already a generous supporter of The Road project. On the night before the event we have a relaxed time and a very classy Lebanese meal, during which, of course, we talk about The Road and Christine offers to attempt to drum up some financial interest for us. If only all 'attempts' turned out like hers!

The following morning we spend time with Bryce Courtenay. He and Iain reminisce about their shared time in Africa. Bryce is extraordinarily buoyant but there are no false heroics. The three of us know this is a farewell. We talk frankly of dying. It is such a relief, for all of us, that there is no pretending. Bryce asks us to have a photograph taken with him, which his wife Christine does.

Then the late afternoon wedding and the next day 800 kilometres back up the highway to our home Here an email awaits from two friends of celebrant Christine, Sidney and Margaret French, people whom we have never met, saying they have deposited $5000 in the Road to Na Lin fund! How incredibly generous and trusting is that!

17

SANTISOUK

In mid-July we are in San Francisco for our daughter's wedding. Held at a function centre in the Presidio, looking out across the Bay and the Golden Gate Bridge, it is totally PERFECTO

Of course I am biased, but Zara looks breathtakingly beautiful. A Great Gatsby look class act in a cream silk retro style full length dress remade to fit her slender frame and height and ultra HIGH heels, her hair simply pulled back and caught in a small gathering of her favorite succulents! Stunning and all set off to perfection by a thirteen-year-old street busker trumpeter, Gabriel, whom she has invited to play her down the 'aisle' it was a stupendous touch.

A week later we are in Laos, once again on our balcony in Luang Prabang, amongst the greenery and silence, recuperating!

James Grindey and Roads Engineer Santisouk Soukasith

On the way from San Francisco, we had stopped off in Vientiane to meet up with James Grindey from the Lao Consulting Group and Santisouk Soukaisith, the Lao engineer who would join us to make a GPS-based assessment of the road into and through NaLin prior to a full survey later.

Santisouk flies with us up to Luang Prabang that same day, to a welcome by Chanthy and the next morning we head off to NaLin, this time by taxi –truck instead of by boat, to the district center of Muang Nan, some 80 kilometers from Luang Prabang, before going on later in the day a further fifteen kilometres or so to NaLin.

Muang Nan is where Chanthy's older brother Jai now lives, though he still does a huge amount of heavy work in his own family's rice fields in NaLin. We stop by the shop-house belonging to Jai's mother-in-law to meet his already pregnant wife Binh. It is also a somewhat private place where we take up Chanthy's polite suggestion that Iain and I change into long trousers, 'more respectful,' he says, for the important meeting we were about to have. Chanthy is our low-key cultural advisor!

The meeting is to be our first with Lao officialdom in the form of an obligatory meeting with the District Roads chap, Vijit Visaipon. He is the Director of Public Works and Transportation for the district that includes NaLin. He wants to meet Santisouk and quiz him about what he plans to do and why. The meeting is also attended by the village headman from NaLin, Dith Chanthamlai and the headmen from two villages Houayhe and Phujong further up the track from NaLin where ethnic minority Khmu and Hmong live. We had not seen these villages on our previous visit to NaLin and were somewhat surprised to learn they were keen to be included in any planned upgrading of the road that, at this time, was really little more than a track.

There is a lot of talk about the type of road they would like, the width, the surface and the number of culverts and what manner of drains, with Santisouk explaining what he thought should be done.

Then comes a question from the Director to Iain and I we would not have expected if Chanthy had not already forewarned us! He asked: 'what do you two want to get from this road to NaLin?'

'Nothing more' Iain replies 'than to see smiles on the faces of the villagers. That's all.'

Road Director Vijit Sisaipon quizzes engineer Santisouk about his plans for a GPS assessment and later survey of the road ... and then us.

The Roads Director nods several times and plays thoughtfully with a large ring on his finger.

From Muang Nan, we swap over into a tok-tok, the only transport that can get into NaLin during the wet and more particularly on this occasion, when the track is in an even worse condition than we had seen it on our previous couple of visits. Oh how much the villagers want and need The Road to be built.

But this time, because of Santisouk's assessment process, after the first day in which we cover the few kilometers of our projected Road To Na Lin, we also plan to follow it a few more kilometers further up into the hills to visit the Khmu and Hmong communities.

Part of the track that will eventually become a road

Santisouk makes a preliminary GPS assessment as a precursor to a full survey

After a night in which we all sleep in a row on the floor, we rise at dawn to travel to these two villages, where Santisouk completes his preliminary assessment work, much of it in heavy rain. It is during this brief extended excursion that Iain and I become aware of the plight of Houayhe and Phujong. These villages are actually far poorer even than NaLin and also in need of help in a score of ways.

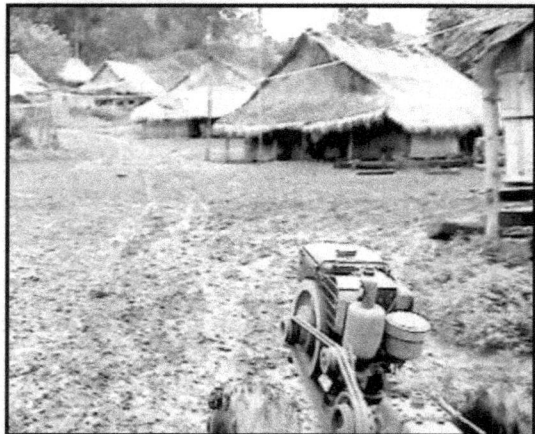

Our first view of the Hmong village of Phujong

It is dark in the one big room of the Phujong village headman's hut, thick with fire smoke from an open hearth in the center of the earthen floor, with several hungry dogs in evidence. The villagers have taken fistfuls of mushrooms from the forest tree trunks and handfuls of weed from a pond they have created off the side of the river to make a welcoming meal for us.

Lunch inside the Hmong Headman's earthen floor hut

The Khmu headman from Houayhe village and the NaLin village headmen are also there. In these impoverished surroundings the Hmong headman, Mr. Laisiew, wears his traditional black loose trousers and jacket edged with a fine hand-sewn trim of red. Handsome, with very distinct Hmong colouring and features, he has been headman for seventeen years and is now forty-five. We work out this means he has guided his people through what must have been a difficult period of transition when, a decade or so ago, the government demanded the Hmong people relocate their villages and come down from high up in the mountains to much lower altitudes.

A man approaches us for help with his ten-year-old son, the same age as our granddaughter, Milla. He holds the boy in his arms as he tells us, 'he can hear, he can speak, he can see, but he cannot walk, because 'his feet are not right...they are bent backwards, from birth'.

There is this touching, heart-breaking belief that because we come from some magic outside place, we have all the answers. If only. He wants to know why this has happened. My god, I think, there are so many possible reasons. He wants to know what can be done to enable the boy to walk.

WARNING: to the next person who says something mealy-mouthed to me about roads bringing drugs/prostitution/21st century social ills to these villages. I will give them a big piece of my mind! Try telling that ignorant nonsense to the boy with the twisted legs, who has no hope of even making a living in the paddy fields, or caring for buffalo and pigs and will live his life literally at dirt floor level trundling about on a homemade trolley.

Back in NaLin, a basi has been organised for Santisouk and when it is over, the villagers all want to ask when, when will The Road be built?

Santisouk speaks quietly but authoritatively

and calmly with all the villagers, trying to explain the mechanical aspects of The Road to them, but clearly emphasizing that when The Road can be built all depends on when the money is available to pay for it all.

And so onward with The Road.

One other incident I want to share: When leaving Muang Nan, on the way back to Luang Prabang by mini-bus, it is necessary about half-way along, to negotiate a long hill that in the pouring rain turns into one long mud-slide. The driver, a young man, but one accustomed to such horrendous weather during the wet and the difficult, if not frightening conditions we are meeting on the way back to Luang Prabang, managed it all with aplomb, gunning the motor and throwing the steering wheel wildly from side to side to get traction for the wheels in the squishy deep mud.

It was a bit hairy and none of us spoke, until I noticed a number of young men, perhaps thirty of them, hunkered down on their haunches on the embankment beside the high side of the track.

'What are they doing?' I ask Chanthy who is naturally surprised that I even need to ask.

'They are waiting to push us,' he explains, 'when we get stuck.'

You notice he said 'when' not 'if'! But we didn't get stuck, thus depriving these stalwart fellows the opportunity of earning, 'How much?' I ask again.

'A few kip only,' Chanthy tells me. 'But during

the wet season they can make enough to pay for school uniforms or books; if they are careful and don't get hurt. Or perhaps to keep for a rainy day.' He smiles self-consciously at being able to joke in English.

The next day, because Chanthy has a few days off work, we plan to all take a bus down to The Plain of Jars, about seven hours bus ride south and out to near where the Americans had their air bases for their Secret War. Chanthy has never been further from his village than Luang Prabang, so he is very excited.

18

THE PLAIN OF JARS

Throughout our developing friendship with Chanthy we have not discussed Lao politics or history. We have not mentioned that we had both worked as journalists in Vietnam during the American/Vietnam War; in my case as a journalist for Singapore newspapers and in Iain's as a foreign correspondent for Australian television and radio.

Nor has it come up that Iain had flown over the Ho Chi Minh Trail and interviewed US Air Force pilots who had carried out bombing raids on that area in eastern Laos during the war. Nor that he had interviewed Prince Souvanna Phouma, leader of the neutralist faction in Laos during the 1950s through 1970s and several times Prime Minister of the former Kingdom of Laos during that period. Souvanna Phouma was a man who spent his entire political life attempting to maintain an even-handed balance between the great powers of East and West, but who ultimately and tragically came to depend on U.S. military aid.

We rationalize this by saying to ourselves: this is not exactly a deceit because all this happened in another age, decades before Chanthy was born and therefore it is not relevant. So our upcoming visit to the Plain of Jars is planned simply as a three-day excursion to see another part of the country and especially to at last get to see the Jars about which we had read so much.

After an 8am start to the bus journey we head south for several hours on a surfaced road which is barely wide enough for vehicles to pass on-coming traffic. Fortunately the driver travels at a steady sensible pace and politely but firmly refuses to engage in chatter with two of the other passengers squashed in beside him, preferring to concentrate on the job at hand.

At the busy, sizeable junction market town of Phu Khun we turn left and head east winding up, up, up into the rugged karst formations of the Annamite Range that forms the Laos/Vietnam border. We enter Xiengkhuang, the province that was so heavily bombarded in the decade between 1964 and 1975 that many small towns and villages were permanently erased and the inhabitants forced to live in caves; more of that later.

At the high pass we stop, joining other busloads of locals at a roadside kitchen in the clouds for a meal of noodles and vegetables and to use the long-drop latrine. Chanthy is in high spirits, lapping up all the new experiences. He phones his parents as we all stand looking out into the mist to tell them about what he is seeing and doing. His enthusiasm is infectious.

A few hours more of winding down, down, down then along the flat of a river valley and we arrive in Phonsavan, a town with the immediate feel of a frontier settlement. The approach streets are wide; large business houses and private homes are set well back on big blocks. The distinctive architecture and pastel colours of the painted bagged brickwork immediately remind us of Vietnam.

Vietnamese faces and language are also very apparent in the street as we make our way to the small hotel where we have made a booking. The Maly Hotel turns out to be a door into both the past and the future.

The past hits us straight in the face as we walk into the small lobby. Clippings from international newspapers and magazines, including front covers of Time and Newsweek magazines line the walls in protective glass cases.

The full gamut of the usual suspects stares out. US Presidents Kennedy, Johnson, Nixon, along with Kissinger, Uncle Ho and U Thant. Coverage by foreign correspondent Stanley Karnow, for whom I worked while living in Hong Kong in the sixties, photographs by Larry Burrows and Horst Fass. Nick Ut's iconic photograph of Kim Phuc, the naked young girl running towards the viewer with her arms held away from the already peeling skin of her napalmed body.

We begin walking along the wall, reading clippings and captions aloud, calling each other's attention to particular people or places. The two young women behind the desk, with whom we have left our passports as required, observe us politely. So does Chanthy, whom we have rudely forgotten in the surprise of falling into a time warp and who has little idea why we are so interested.

I stop drinking all this in for long enough to try explaining to Chanthy things about his own country's past and how some of these people fit in. But then Iain lets out a cry of excitement, 'Come and look at this.' He is leaning over a glass cabinet, inside which are shelves laden with hardcover books. On the top shelf is a book, open at its frontispiece that is crammed with the flamboyant signatures of men whose names are known to us.

'They're all Ravens'.

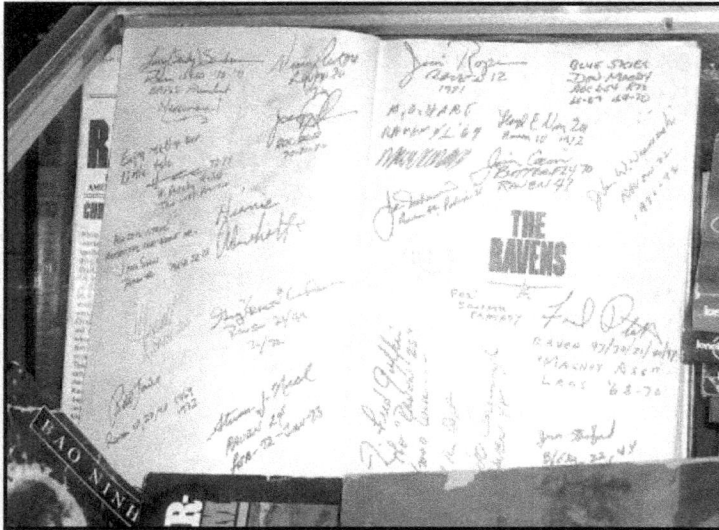

A copy of Christopher Robins book *The Ravens* adorned with the signatures of the mercenary pilots of Laos' Secret War

These are the signatures of the men who flew in the secret air war over Laos. This book, *The Ravens* and another, *Air America*, both by British author, Christopher Robbins, that we have only recently read, give candid details about the operation of the CIA's clandestine airline, Air America, as well as the motivation and casual insouciance of a separate, but also CIA-funded group of highly paid mercenary pilots, the *Ravens*. This is the name taken by the men who flew the spotter planes that guided US air-force fighter-bombers in dropping tons of bombs, napalm and cluster bombs along the Ho Chi Minh Trail, killing in the process, in addition to their military enemies, uncounted numbers of civilian men, women and children.

The sliding glass doors of the bookcase are locked and as we stand up from a vain attempt to jiggle them open, two things happen simultaneously; we come face to face with the past in the form of a large colour photograph of a man in the full dress white uniform and medals of a general. 'I think that's Soth Phetrasy', the spokesman for the communist Pathet Lao forces during the war, Iain says, just as the future comes through the front door in the form of a young man who confirms our thoughts: 'Yes,' he says, '...it *is* General Phetrasy and I am his grandson, Vilan Phetrasy.'

There is pride in the way he speaks his name. Phetrasy is a name to conjure with in Laos. 'They tell me,' he gestures towards the women behind the desk, 'that you want to have a look around and that you ask a lot of questions.'

Over an excellent dinner eaten in the hotel's cozy dining room whose walls are 'decorated' with bomb casings, fearsome man-traps, once hidden on jungle footpaths, old and rusty AK47s, de-fused cluster bombs, and handmade flags, we talk with Chanthy about the Secret War, the America/Vietnam War, Lao history, colonialism and the politics of south east Asia.

Most of it is news to him and he asks a lot of heartbreakingly basic questions. For all his life, his immediate family has had their work cut out just barely managing to keep their heads above the waterline of starvation. The same goes for the villagers he grew up around. The education system is pretty light on when it comes to anything much more than the three Rs. It's a lot for him to grapple with.

Its been a long, full day and we take advantage of having serendipitously fallen in with Vilan, who not only owns and manages the Maly Hotel, but offers to spend the whole of the next day taking us on a tour of the Plain of Jars

Chanthy had told us, even before we left Luang Prabang, he didn't want to sleep in a room on his own. He has never done that. He is afraid of ghosts. These are not ghosts like you and I might use the description, they are *phii,* spirits and we came to appreciate that the link, indeed the cross over between the everyday world and that of the *phii* is a very loosely woven web.

Apparently *phii* are all around us all the time and not just at night. But night is when the mind is more receptive to them. Not all of them have bad intentions, indeed it is said there are many good *phii*. Trouble is it is hard to tell the goodies from the baddies at first. That's my fairly loose take on this not quite separate Laotian world!

So we all sleep in the one big room with three beds and share the one bathroom. Chanthy tells us, in the disarmingly frank manner that is his nature, 'this is the first time I ever sleep in a bed and the first time I ever have a hot shower in a separate room.' We just hope that these pleasurable experiences are enough to keep the *phii* of the horrors we have talked about over dinner from invading his nighttime mind.

A large part of the following morning we spend out on the Plain of Jars, which is just that; an undulating high plain, dotted with many hundreds of stone jars varying in size from a flower pot to something that could quite easily contain a couple of fairytale Ali Babas.

'Be careful not to stray from the marked path,' Vilan warns us. 'This entire area is still heavily seeded with *bombies*.'

Indeed we pass close by several small teams of men, all wearing orange overalls, searching for UXO with sensitive handheld equipment.

Vilan Pethrasy on the Plain of Jars

Bomb disposal experts still at work almost 40 years after the end of the Viet Nam War

Vilan has already shown us what 'bombies' look like and graphically described the hideous damage they can inflict. As mentioned earlier, the film about Laith Stevens, the mine expert, we had seen at the Rotary Club function, told how fifty years after this part of Lao was carpet-bombed by the Americans, roughly 100 people, mostly inquisitive, fearless young children are maimed every year by UXO. Forty a year die from their injuries. Between 1964 and 2008 fifty thousand people, almost all of them civilians, have been killed by UXO. These figures are given on the trustworthy *Legacies of War* website.

The Geneva Convention now outlaws cluster bombs. But that has not prevented their use in the myriad conflicts that continue to erupt around the world; most recently Syrian government forces have been shown to be using them. In all circumstances they are employed not so much against armed military personnel but rather to terrorize civilian populations.

Huge mysterious stone jars litter the plain

The jars we have come to see may also themselves be the result of war. It has been suggested that the biggest, perhaps weighing 6 tonnes, is the victory cup of a mythical King Jeuam. There are also other suggestions: that they were created, almost all of them from a type of sandstone, as sarcophagi, or for fermenting wine, or for rice storage. Some are decorated. The majority of them are plain. Some have lids. Most do not. Estimated to be some 2000 years old, they remain an enigma in large part because archaeological investigation has been slowed by many years of war and the very significant danger of unexploded ordnance.

As we follow the narrow, well-defined safety path we pick up on snatches of Vilan's, until very recently, fractured life; an unwitting product of his country's splintered history. With his own mother dying at a young age, Vilan spent much of his early childhood living with his grandmother and grandfather General Phetrasy, who represented the new Lao government in numerous world capitals. Vilan obviously has an innate talent for language and during these years he mastered quite number of disparate ones, including Chinese, Thai and English. He exhibits some of the telltale signs of a childhood spent on the move but mostly he has managed to turn these to his advantage.

Settled back in Laos, Vilan rejoined his father, Sousath, who had remarried and had a daughter, Maly, after whom the hotel is named. Sousath, himself deeply emotionally scarred by his participation in and knowledge of the Secret War, eventually found some form of healing strength by working on a plan to begin clearing the UXO and to bring the Plain of Jars to world attention as a tourist destination. He certainly achieved that aim, although he was destined to die in his late fifties.

Following his father's death Vilan spent two years as a novice living in a wat. When he rejoined the wider community it was to take up the burdensome joy of continuing with his father's vision.

We ask him to take some happy snaps of

Chanthy and us. Chanthy, who we can see is grappling with all this historical and personal information, is wearing a sports shirt emblazoned across the front with a man on water-skis and the word Tumbulgum. That's the name of our nearest village back home. Hannah and Geoff, the young couple who run the general store and post office there, are going through the usual struggles involved in putting two sons through high-school. They have been given an earful about The Road to NaLin and just before we came away, in a generous gesture they gave us four of these shirts as presents for the villagers. We had chosen the smallest sizes, but even these all but drowned members of the Sisombuth family and water-skiing had proved difficult to explain.

Vilan drives us, surprisingly carefully, in his big four-wheel drive, the obligatory vehicle if you are to get around in Xiengkhuang Province especially in the wet season. We visit a small village where bomb casings have been rehabilitated: for use as support columns for a house, a dovecote, a veggie planter box, a fence line and even beaten into sickles and knives.

Bomb casings
support a dovecote
in a Plain of Jars
village

He disappears into one of the raised huts and returns to tell us, 'the people I wanted you to meet have gone away for a wash in the river.' He elaborates that they are two Australian couples, who of their own accord and with their own monies are here on the Plain of Jars, building simple ablution facilities; piping water up from the river, building a shower stall and long a drop toilet; more members of the Laos Underground.

We drive on, with me having lost whatever there was of a sense of direction and finally come to a halt in a vast, open, treeless valley. Vilan gets out and strides off. We follow. There are a small number of buffaloes grazing around a series of large indentations in the land.

A bomb crater in 'B-52 alley' on the Ho Chi Minh Trail

'Bomb craters,' Vilan explains. 'Look there.' With our eyes we follow the direction of his gesture. 'That is the way they came, the B52s, dropping their bombs as they flew. It seems there was no particular target, although there may have been troops here at the time. Maybe they were just short on fuel and wanted to lessen their payload. Who knows? Who will ever know?'

For as far as you can see and beyond that, there are bomb craters like the one we are standing beside. 'The entire valley was set ablaze. Nothing and nobody survived. Even now only grass grows. No trees or even shrubs.'

He scuffs at the earth with his hiking boot, then bends down, 'see this, it's a piece of bomb casing.' He drops into Iain's open palm a piece of twisted and buckled rusted metal two or three centimeters long.' Rubbing at it we turn it around in hands. 'Can I keep this?' Iain asks. 'Of course,' Vilan says, 'there's plenty more here.' That piece of metal is now held secure by a sliver of silver and I wear it as a memento-mori necklace.

After a brief stop for rice and noodles during which its impossible not to notice the majority of the stallholders are Vietnamese and that Chanthy is noticeable subdued, we take off to visit another village. Recent rains have swelled the river so this involves squelching through deep mud and hand-hauling ourselves across a rickety bamboo bridge.

A woman with great poise, who exudes natural leadership, welcomes us cheerfully. As we follow her up a steep ladder into her one room home, Vilan explains she is the head of the village women's committee and responsible for organizing their weaving project from woe to go. In the dim interior light we meet some of the weavers who show us their handicrafts, all hand-woven from locally grown cotton and silk and coloured with natural dyes. They kneel down and squatting back on their heels spread before us a largess of beauty. Of course we purchase some, wishing only that we had more room in our small travel bags.

Beautiful textiles from a small and impoverished village on the Plain of Jars

Back downstairs, between the teak stilts on which the house stands we inspect the heavy solid looms these women deftly manipulate into creating these miniature shimmering masterpieces and Vilan tells of yet another of his imaginative plans. 'I have put together a group of about forty blind women from all over Xiengkhuang Province who can weave. Yes. Weave. They have become dexterous enough to distinguish between the various textures of threads, on the one hand, by touch. But what is even more extraordinary is that, because the natural dyes are all made from plants and seeds they can also tell the colours by their smell.' He smiles as we express our amazement. 'They weave amazingly intricate patterns.'

'These are women who are blind due to the effects of Agent Orange. The soil in large areas of the Province was so drenched by this chemical defoliant during the war that it can never recover. It was common for women who were pregnant at the time of the bombing to give birth to children with massive deformities, including blindness. For unknown reasons this blindness has reoccurred in the next and even following generations.'

'We already have the transportation and sales infrastructure in place through having established weaving in this village. So all we need to do is build two looms, from local teak, because that is long lasting in this climate. We would need one simple room to accommodate all the women and basic kitchen and toilet facilities. I think it can all be done for sixty thousand dollars.' Vilan smiles.

'When you go back to your home, tell people about this. Ask for help. You would know how helping women is the best way of helping the whole community.'

So there you go. How about it? See, treasured opportunities sometime just drop into your lap.

After a less than refreshing dip in a mineral hot springs whose muddy water has been channeled through bamboo pipes into an elbow in the river, we head off to the last venue for the day. Tham Piu cave. This place could not exactly be described as a tourist attraction.

'I won't come up with you,' Vilan tells us as he parks the car in the shade at the base of the cliff at whose top we can see a cave entrance: 'Too many spirits. But please, light a candle for me up there. I'll stay here and join in the football.' Chanthy clenches his teeth. 'You should look in the museum first and take a torch' Vilan suggests before going off to join in with a spontaneous team of likely lads who are kicking a ball about on a field designated by a tee shirt here, a baseball cap there.

The little one-room museum displays gruesome photographs of charred and melted bodies and details the names of almost three hundred men, women and children who were incinerated in a nano-second when a US war plane fired a single rocket into the cave in the last month of 1968.

Tam Pui Cave: site of a US rocket attack that killed 300.

The walls of the enormous cave that stretch back into the darkness are deeply stained. I recall my stepmother talking about the firebombing of air-raid shelters in her hometown of Hamburg and how all that was left was the cooked grease of human bodies. Chanthy and I stay near the mouth while Iain explores further into the interior. We light candles and look out over the treetops into the green beyond. We don't talk because words are inadequate.

19

TEMPORARY NOVICES

On our last evening at the Maly Hotel we all watched the film *The Most Secret Place on Earth,* the same movie we had watched with the Rotary group back in Australia. What we had not known at that time was that it was Vilan's father, Sousath, who took the filmmakers to Long Chen, the secret town of some 50,000 people during the late sixties and early seventies. It remained hidden from world view in the jungle-clad mountains to the south-west of Phonsavan throughout the Vietnam War. The film includes interviews with CIA and Air America officials as well as with Vang Pao the Hmong General who led an army of his people to battle against the Viet Cong and North Vietnamese soldiers who were infiltrating Laos along the Ho Chi Minh Trail. These Hmong hill-people were vilified and discriminated against after the eventual takeover by the communist government in Laos in

1975.

Nobody comes out of the film as one hundred percent lovable.

Back in Luang Prabang, over a meal of Ms. Er's fish laap and green mango salad, we talk with Chanthy about the visit to Phonsavan, the Plain of Jars and the conversations with Vilan Phetrasy.

'I prefer to live in Luang Prabang,' Chanthy says quietly. 'I enjoy seeing it all and I learn a lot,' he adds, politely letting us know he appreciated the opportunity of the visit, 'but there are too many Vietnamese and it has no heart.' We think he is referring to Phonsavan being spread out, having no obvious bustling centre as in Luang Prabang, but then he adds, 'I saw no monks and only one wat.'

There had been so much movement and so many happenings, we had not yet told Chanthy about the proposed visit to Laos of the Broadbeach Rotarians. We ask him whether he thought it would be possible to organize for them to visit NaLin and explain this is important, as we hope they will put some funds into helping to build The Road.

He immediately takes positively to the idea and by the time we see him on the next day he has already phoned his Dad about the visit and been told that a boat, a tok-tok and a basi can be organised. Over the next few days we check out boutique hotels with the type of required facilities.

On a separate mission we also go for what has

become the annual visit to Phosi market to stock up on clothing and books for Chanthy and his sister Bounlee for the upcoming school year.

Our days now, generally begin with a leisurely cycle alongside the Mekong River, exchanging greetings with people who are sweeping the streets and pavements and setting up their cafés for the breakfast trade and who have come to recognize us as part of the scenery. Most of them would probably also know we are houseguests of Noi and his family. Nothing stays secret for long in Luang Prabang.

Down past the former Royal Palace now museum and the early morning market; crowded as always with bleary-eyed western visitors transported in from outlying swish hotels. They come en-masse in the sort of linked-together, electric-powered open carriages of the type one sees trundling about in theme parks.

Sometimes there are funerals underway; highly decorated coffins with photographs of the deceased adorned with garlands of marigolds under a gold paper panoply. Long tables are set for a constantly changing flow of family and friends who seamlessly eat, talk, play cards and watch television. These expensive formalities can go on for several days, depending on how long the wait is for the crematorium that is situated at a wat on the far side of the Nam Khan River.

A bit of a pull on the bikes up the rise beside the series of French built government offices, now occupied by the army and outside which young men perform their early morning routine ablutions and where there is also always a young soldier practicing on his guitar. Then around the rather ugly fountain, a dancing figure made of decaying cracked cement, from which water never spouts. Back we pedal through the middle of the town, where tourists are starting to have their breakfasts and making plans for their day visits to the waterfall, the Buddha cave, or a wander through a few of the thirty-three wats which are the raison d'être for Luang Prabang.

We sight orange-robed Khamchanh, accompanied by a small acolyte, both walking towards the Monk's School. We wave and he inclines his head. When we see him later in the day, he tells us that an American woman has sponsored him to attend the American University in Vientiane and that he has applied for a place there. This means leaving the wat, his home for the last seven years. Naturally he is excited and anxious in equal part.

He tells us there will be a fair and market happening this coming weekend at the outskirts and town and he would like to meet us there. He is very pleased when we suggest that we would like to help ease him into his new life and that he may like to choose some clothing at the inevitable accompanying Vietnamese-run stalls.

It turns out to be quite an experience, but only for Iain because, knowing it would not be the done thing for a female to accompany a monk or novice on a clothes-shopping expedition, I hang back at the entrance to the makeshift market. This leaves Iain to go with Khamchanh, who is dressed of course in his robes, as they wander from stall to stall looking at clothing.

Iain tells me later: 'Stallholders made no concession to the fact that Khamchanh is a novice. They quoted outrageous prices for the shirts, shorts and sneakers he chose and he thought that was the fixed price. He hadn't a clue about bargaining and was amazed when I stepped in and did it for him. The traders were equally surprised when I turned out to be his friend and that I was paying for the purchases. Of course he couldn't try anything on and he had no idea about sizes for any of it so I estimated as accurately as I could and then I told them, 'we'll take this, this and this, I'll leave a deposit and he will try these things on at his wat and we'll come back later this afternoon with what we have chosen, pay for that and give you back what we don't want.' Some of the tee shirts he looked at were totally not right. I told him, 'you need ones with collars, nothing too bright and no slogans. And you need long trousers and proper shoes.'

Because we have had three longtime friends die this year and with others seemingly on the way out, we visit our nearest wat, Wat Xiengthong, the oldest in town, established in 1560 before Australia was even a twinkle in a white-fellow's eye. It is just over the laneway from our home in Khoumxiengthong Guest House. We light candles and burn some incense in an atmosphere of deep serenity.

Farewelling friends in Luang Prabang's oldest temple, Wat Xiengthong

We walk back into the grounds of the guesthouse where Noi's wife Thiemchanh, who not so mysteriously knows where we have been and what we have been doing, meets us. She smiles gently and gives us a plate of honey soaked bananas and grated coconut wrapped in leaves.

'My sons will become novices next week,' she tells us.

'All of them? All at once?' We must sound surprised.

She inclines her head. 'The three of them, for a week. There will be a special ceremony, for family and friends and you would be welcome to join us if you would like.' We realize it is an honour to be asked and yes, indeed, we would like very much to attend.

Chanthaek, Chanthaboun and Chantaphone about to become novices for a week

For the induction process, the three young men have their heads and eyebrows ceremonially shaved at home, during which process there is quite a deal of informal joshing. They are also carefully dressed in new white robes by their male relatives, before heading off in a family procession to Wat Souvannakhizi, also just across Sisavangyong Road from the guest house. The temple is packed with a number of social A-listers and political powers that be that I recognize from that first wedding as well as family and neighbours. In the middle of a row of monks, sitting cross-legged on the floor, an older one, clearly the most senior, is leading the Pali chanting with responses from this congregation. There is some silent praying and much reverential bowing, heads to the floor.

Lots of local children hang around the doorways hoping to get a glimpse of the doings and perhaps score some candy and soft drinks.

The three lads are still wearing their diaphanous white robes, with very apparent bright-coloured board shorts beneath But about an hour into the ceremony, they are led out into the wat grounds where assistant monks discreetly help them into the complex folds of their new orange robes before returning inside the wat for more invocations from the senior monks who sit cross-legged, waiting silently for their return.

The three boys return in orange robes for the closing parts of the induction process

For fifteen minutes or so the senior monk reads an invocation from a text and then there is a brief period of chanting from both the gathered guests and the three monks, which signals the end of the public proceedings, following which the boys move off into the monastry for a week.

A privileged experience for us. Back at the guesthouse we join the family and relatives for noodle soup prepared by Thiemchanh.

Every morning for the next week, as we set off on our habitual early morning cycle, we see Thiemchanh kneeling at the roadside waiting with other local women to place alms of food in the proffered bowls of the novices as they stream silently by. Among them are her three sons.

20

SUDDENLY $10,000!!

We sit at our computers on our cool green balcony aerie from which we admire the immaculate garden next door while Iain continues to finalize plans via email and phone for our family celebration of my seventieth birthday, in a few months time in Shanghai. It is an embarrassing self-indulgence. But we have always our marked our decade-turnings with special events as one never knows whether there'll be an opportunity to celebrate another.

On the morning of our departure for home Chanthy presents himself to us like the cat that's caught the mouse: with a grin from ear to ear.

'I have a surprise for DearTrishDearIain,' he announces, handing us both carefully wrapped parcels. He watches with pleasure as we unwrap beautiful hand-woven scarves made from cotton, coloured in various shades of blue for me, browns for Iain, using natural dyes.

'This is first time I can give a present,' he beams. 'They come from my shop. Made by minority hill tribe people and they become softer with each washing.' We smile at his learnt sales patter. He has been quick to learn what it is westerners want to hear about the products he sells.

On the way to the airport, which no longer holds the awe for him it did the first time he waved us off, he points out the area where his Aunt, Thongmee Phonevilai, his Great-Aunt in our terminology, has a simple house on a small piece of land. 'When I finish schooling, get a good job, get married and have children, I will buy a piece of land from her and build the house I showed you the toy of in NaLin. You remember?'

We do indeed remember the maquette he had shown us of his dream house. 'Bit by bit, step by step,' he smiles at us repeating the mantra as applying to everything in life.

The view from the window of the plane on the flight south to the capital reveals the full extent of the dramatic all-but uncultivable geography of the country and Iain spends the hour regaling me with stories of his first flight on this route, piloted by a gung-ho Laotian air-force officer during which barrels of live fish were packed in the aisles: also with unrepeatable stories of his young man wild escapades in the then loose-living war-zone capital. The Vientiane into which we now descend is a comparatively sedate place, though perhaps only on the surface.

We check into Sala Inpeng, the low-key one-story residence set in a tropical garden where we always feel at home and in the morning take a tuk-tuk ride the short distance out to the little piece of Australia on the edge of town. There is an anaesthetic cleanliness about the modern lines of the Embassy's stark whiteness but Lynda Worthaisong, Australia's Ambassador to The Lao People's Democratic Republic, is warm, personable and shows enthusiastic interest in our Road to Na Lin project.

With Ambassador Lynda Worthaisong and Mone Sysavath

Mone Sysavath from the Australian Aid Agency, AusAid, joins the meeting and is equally supportive. He knows of the Lao Consulting Group, the company of which James Grindey is manager and for which Santisouk, the Lao roads engineer who made the GPS assessment of the roads into and out of NaLin village, works.

We mention that we have just met in Muang Nan with Vijit Visaipon, Director of the Department of Public Works and Transportation for Nan District. That too is well received as Mone also knows of him.

I ask Lynda how she feels about working for the Foreign Affairs Department. Her spontaneous response is obviously genuine. 'I love it. I wake up every day thinking how fortunate I am, looking forward to going to work and hoping the day will bring an opportunity to make a difference for the better.'

Sometimes one feels that our tax dollars are going to the right people.

At the offices of the Lao consulting group we are hoping to meet up again with James Grindey but as he is out of town on a work project, we arrange to get together with only Santisouk. We explain to him that we would like to get something on paper about his recent assessment and the upcoming survey as soon as possible as we need something concrete to show the RNL Committee and our donors back home. He gives us the first and very preliminary report and a map.

We know that the next two months at home in Australia are going to be tight-packed so we hit the floor running by arranging to have a RNL Committee Meeting combined with luncheon on our deck two days after getting back. We need to bring Marty and wife Ally, Phil and his Sikkimese wife

Ongmu, up to speed with all the good news.

We also start immediately into assisting John and Marilyn Bee in getting the best experience possible out of their upcoming two-week visit to Laos with twelve members of Broadbeach Rotary Club.

It is arranged that Chanthy will accompany John Bee to the morning market to purchase the food necessary for the village to put on a basi ceremony. He will also take a day off work to go downriver with them as their guide and interpreter, unpaid, of course. Nevertheless, Chanthy feels a bit nervous. He's anxious because he doesn't have an official government-issued guide's license. But we assure him that as he is not being paid for these services, he can honestly announce himself to any nosey-parker official as simply a friend of John Bee.

An unpleasant sticking point occurs, because Iain and I have unknowingly underpriced the riverboat for travel downriver to NaLin via the riverside village of Hadsaikham. Iain explains to John that Chanthy has advised us that since the last time we used the boat the price of fuel has greatly increased and that instead of the $100 we first mentioned to him as being what we had paid for our river trip eighteen months previously, the skipper is now charging $150. It is a big boat, for thirty to forty passengers, so he is charging the price he would normally collect from a boatload of paying passengers. For twelve people, the price is now roughly $12.50 instead of just over $8.00 each.

In retrospect and in the light of later events,

perhaps the kindest thing that can be said is that John is perhaps stressed by the planning and organising of a trip for twelve people, as he suggests this increase in the fee for the boat is an indication that Chanthy is attempting to rip him off. Just as well it is Iain and not me who is doing the phone negotiations because I may well have spoken my mind and then hung up. An extra $3.50 per person for the trip of a lifetime on the mighty Mekong. I think these were the very words I shouted at Iain who phoned John and told him, 'Trish and I will pay the extra $50 ourselves.'

Chanthy, stuck between the boat owner, the villagers who can see the importance of the Rotary visit and us must have had second thoughts about his role as negotiator. But he remained unflappable and always polite.

In a full-on fuzz-ball of activities there are a number of memorable standouts.

We drive a hundred William Shatner biographies up to Trekkie Mary Kemp in Brisbane. In the unlikely setting of a small church car-park we exchange books for cash and get to meet a group of her fellow Trekkies who somehow or other manage to emanate an aura of other-worldly weirdness.

We are asked to become 'god-parents' and to give an Australian name to Jai and Binh's son, Chanthy's nephew, who is now three months old and considered to have survived the most dangerous period and made a claim on life. We put considerable time and thought into this but cannot come up with anything better than Sydney, which may be unimaginative but is very Australian.

A direct approach to the ANZ Bank whose TV ads are fulsome in praising their commitment to our Asian neighbours is knocked back and we glumly come to accept that only we will build The Road to NaLin.

Then suddenly, Dick and Pip Smith drop a further TEN THOUSAND DOLLARS into the fund! and we get to make up our first Diamond Certificate to send them, along with a big, big thank you.

Another huge boost from Dick and Pip Smith: $10,000 !

As always in life, everything happens at once. A date is arranged by James Grindey for Santisouk to follow through on his preliminary assessment by doing a full survey during September. On James' advice we send an upfront payment of $3000, as half payment for the work, through to Lao Consulting. In Skype conversations and emails with

Chanthy we ask him to make sure that lots of photographs are taken of this work in progress.

Naturally no one in the village has a camera but Chanthy arranges to borrow one from the inevitable cousin and send it down by bus and tok-tok to his Dad. 'We need photographs of the work being done,' Iain pushes, 'not people standing in group shots.'

It seems as if nothing fazes Chanthy, this village lad who fell in with a couple of foreigners and whose life has since been turned upside down. 'I will tell this to my father,' he assures us.

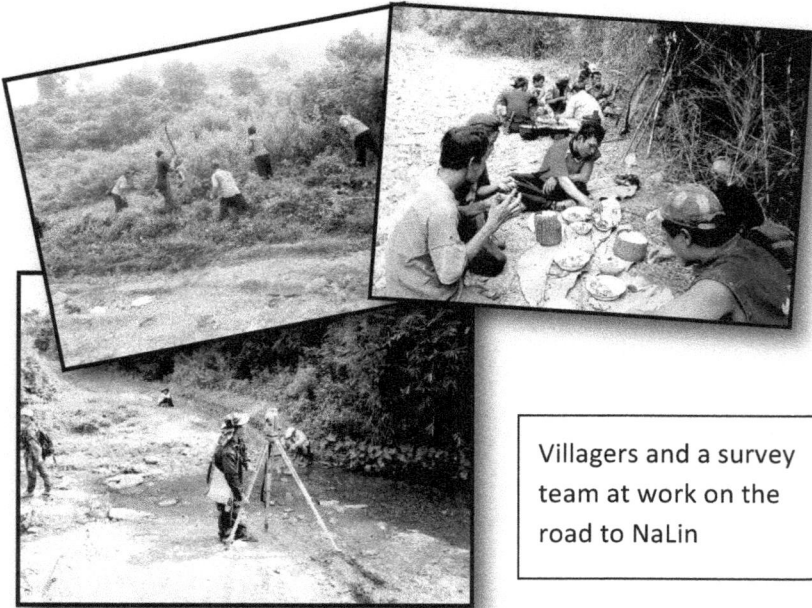

Villagers and a survey team at work on the road to NaLin

He must have because the 20 or so photographs are exactly what we need. They show groups of villagers assisting Santisouk by cutting down rampant foliage, taking measurements with theodolytes and also having a simple meal spread out on banana leaves on the track, with the engineer and his professional colleagues all hunkered down around them eating.

We receive the pictures by email a couple of weeks later, shortly after our arrival in Shanghai, for my November birthday get-together

21

HELP FROM THE COMMUNISTS!

Celebrating my three score years and ten with family and friends in Shanghai, on the tenth floor of the historic Peace, formerly Cathay, Hotel overlooking the Bund was utterly memorable.

We followed this up by travelling independently as a twosome through Myanmar and that too was an incredible experience. But as John Lennon's memorable quote confirms, 'Life is what happens while you're busy making other plans.' And the truth of this hit us with tremendous force as we left Yangon.

The overnight flight is a blur of disconnect and both of us all but fell off the plane and headed to the doctor where our own earlier self-diagnosis of giardia was confirmed. We were informed that the heavy-duty anti-biotic Flagyl was required and in significantly large doses.

We made it home, where kind neighbours had stocked up the fridge and for four days lay about at what we fancifully imagined was death's door.

That a minute waterborne parasite can create such havoc in the human body is a lesson in size being totally unimportant and in the vulnerable fragility of the human body. Violent, explosive diarrhea, nausea, cramps, immense thirst, a foul metallic taste in the mouth, an unremitting headache and utterly total lethargy left us both barely able to function let alone think about The Road to NaLin.

The disease is named after the French zoologist, Alfred Mathieu Giard, who first discovered its cause. I would prefer to give my name to a new variety of rose.

At the first sign of respite, Iain managed to get together, print and mail our annual end of year card, with which we always mark the passing seasons. Our grandchildren came for a bush and beach holiday and for an all too brief ten days it felt as though it was going to be one of those glorious long hot summers of memory. The ocean creek was a paradise for our daily swims.

Then Cyclone Oswald came through, shredded the landscape and left us isolated us and without power for four days. Fortunately our small acreage and buildings suffered no major damage.

We were still mopping up when I was kneecapped by what at first I dismissed as a summer cold but which, with frightening rapidity, developed into a chest-tearing, mad dog barking cough.

Glossing over details, because other people's wordy obsession with what one elderly good pal describes as the 'daily organ recital' is tedious, we finally became concerned enough to have a range of tests including an x-ray and blood tests. The totally unsuspected diagnosis was Legionnaires' Disease.

A fairly large-scale shock at this news and then more medications, powerful antibiotics and rest, rest, rest. Total bodily self-obsession. A very demanding patient. Though once I persuade myself to relax into the inevitable, I read heaps and do a lot of thinking. We decline all visitors. I am not up to speed even for phone calls or emails.

I learn a lot, both about myself as well as others and when I finally come up for air after more than six weeks, it is not exactly as a new woman but, yes, a different person.

The Road is waiting, with both bad and good news.

The bad news is no news. No news or even contact throughout this period from the Bees or anyone else from Broadbeach Rotary. Iain gets in touch with Peter Gowans, an ex-ABC cameraman who had gone on the Rotary visit to NaLin and who had promised to shoot some footage of their time there, that he would be able to share with us. He is disappointed to be told by Peter that he'd had trouble downloading his movie footage. Apparently it is all lost and non-recoverable.

But our disappointment over this is more than compensated for by the extra-good news that, following our meeting six months previously with Vijit Visaiphon, District Director of the Department of Public Works and Transportation and our offer of providing him with the detailed survey we had organised with Santisouk, the road engineer in September the Public Works Department had allocated some 500 million kip, the equivalent of around $70,000 to upgrade the track through to the minority villages of Houayhe and Phujong including, we assumed, NaLin.

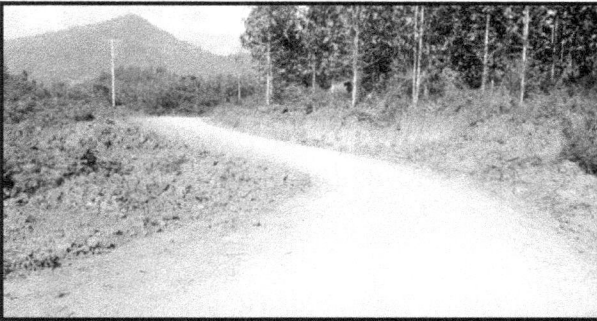

New government work on the Road to Houayhe and Phujong villages

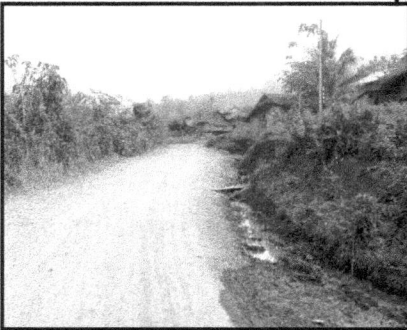

The work had been carried out during December just after we had arrived back in Australia. With this enormous boost from

the Lao Government, it appears we're at last getting somewhere...However it also seems that the actual road into, through and beyond NaLin village has not benefitted from the government upgrade, largely we feel, because the Government is aware we are planning to cover the work on this section.

So this is not a signal to sit back on our laurels and relax. We still need to spread the word about The Road so as to raise as much funding as possible. To that end we need to stand out from the crowd expected to be vying for attention at Royal Pines Resort on the Gold Coast where Rotary District 9640 is holding their annual convention. This means we need to put together yet another version of our videos and for this we need to pull together more facts and figures, track down photographs of culverts and drains and shoot some more pieces to camera.

Good news comes in the form of the announcement of the birth of Vilan Phetrasy's baby, a boy who is given the western name of David. We are again honoured to be asked to become David's god-parents.

Chanthy's sister Bounlee is completing the second and final year of her fulltime training as a Kindergarten Teacher. In order to graduate she is required to spend three months in a hands-on situation in a distant southern province. Having never been out from under the protective wing of either her parents on their farm or Chanthy in Luang Prabang, this is her first exposure to independence and the bigger world and she is naturally anxious; though not as anxious as her parents and touchingly, her brother. We send supportive emails and follow her progress with the apprehension of surrogate parents.

But Bounlee is obviously a brave chip off the old block and settles in easily and happily with the family with whom she is officially boarded. After six weeks Mum and Dad travel down by bus and truck to visit and although she is naturally homesick, she has taken to teaching like a duck to water.

A piece of housekeeping pops up for attention. In order to remain a legal entity with *Communities New South Wales*, that is to retain a licence to raise funds for a charitable cause, we need our accounts to be audited. Fortunately our accountant in Murwillumbah generously does this somewhat detailed work for free. Thankyou, enthusiastic canoeist, Brian Meldrum

As the Rotary event looms ever closer we also need to make posters and flyers with information about The Road as well as ourselves that also includes a fill-in and tear-off invitation, asking us to visit the such-and-such Rotary Club in order to tell them about our project. Rotary Distict 9640 covers almost sixty clubs over a diverse area from south of Brisbane to Grafton and from the coast out to Goondawindi. If every one of those clubs wanted to hear about The Road... dream on Trish dream on... we'd need to get our skates on!

We also need to make copies of Iain's DVD and print off DVD labels. Maps, flags, blutack, drawing pins, cashbox and receipt book (positive thinking!), electronic wizardry such as cables, jacks and monitors and as always my trusty sarong, all this needs to be ticked off the list as it goes into big plastic carry boxes.

If only plans eventuated the way you designed them!

22

A CONTRACTOR

During the week leading up to the Rotary Convention we receive a phone call from John Bee. There had been no thank you card (foolish thought Trish) or even email thanking us for the sizeable amount of assistance we had given them in organizing what surely must have been the highlight of their visit to Lao; their voyage on the Mekong and their visit to NaLin. Now, four months later, this call out of the blue.

It appears they have heard we would be setting up a booth at the upcoming Rotary Convention. John told Iain that he and Marilyn would have a booth there too. They had not previously mentioned this Convention to us, let alone suggested there might be a way of our project benefitting from it. It would seem it's dog eat dog out there even in the world of charity.

'We would have liked to hear how your visit to NaLin went,' says Iain with only the slightest edge to his tone. So it is arranged that we meet for a meal at their local Thai restaurant. The food is excellent but my tolerance for their lack of any real interest in our project has worn thin. Neither of them ask about how fund-raising for The Road is progressing, nor about Chanthy, his family and the other NaLin villagers who had shown them and their group such hospitality. They had made no such intimate connections.

When it comes time to pay the bill for the meal Iain somewhat jocularly reminds them of his offer, prior to their visit to NaLin. When John had become stroppy about the $50 increase in the fee for the Mekong river boat hire and even voiced his opinion that Chanthy was trying to rip him off, Iain had said we ourselves would pay the extra $50, which spread across the twelve Rotarians would have come out at less than $5 each. So now, we do just that by paying for their meal as well as our own. Neither John nor Marilyn demur.

Our booth at the Rotary Convention

The following weekend it's the Rotary Convention. Firm believers in the early bird catching the worm, by 7am we have set up our booth: posters, sarongs, prayer flags, flyers and video loop.

John Bee and two of the other members of Broadbeach Rotary who visited NaLin, arrive shortly after. Later, during a break in proceedings, when their booth is left unattended, I see they have a heart-rending, poster-sized photograph of the young Hmong boy-child whom I had mentioned to the doctors who were going to be travelling as part of their group.

The boy has completely paralysed or at least non-functioning legs. We knew through Chanthy that his father had brought him down on a tok-tok from the Hmong village of Phujong. We had mentioned that there would be at least one doctor among the visiting Rotarians and we had hoped there was something positive could be done for the lad.

Now here is this large-scale photograph being used to attract attention to the Bee's booth. If something positive had happened or if there had been some sort of follow-up on the boy by the Rotarian doctors or the Bees, it would not have been so bad, but there had been nothing. The boy, his father, in fact nobody in NaLin village or Phujong heard any more from the group of Broadbeach Rotarians they had welcomed.

Later it emerges that John and Marilyn Bee are planning to move to Laos to set up a tour business operation. Poverty Tourism. They do so before the end of the year. We feel foolish and used and worst of all distressed for the villagers.

However, the positive side of the convention is meeting Deborah Ralf, who has a booth across from us and whom we sense, before we even introduce ourselves, lives life to the max and on the edge. She's a Rotary Volunteer and teaches sewing and other useful life skills to illegal refugee women in Mae Sot, a frontier town on the Thai/Myanmar border where anything goes including people trafficking, child labour, child prostitution and jade, sapphire and teak wood smuggling. Deborah is a one-person aid organization working under the auspices of SAW a Burmese group that cares for displaced, trafficked, abused and HIV/AIDS-affected women and children from Myanmar. Rotary Australia World Community Service (RAWCS) is her umbrella and safety net.

'Since I was sixteen I have always done volunteer work because I had a keen sense of the huge divide between the haves and the have-nots. I have always believed that one person can make a difference,' she tells me in her appealingly scatter-shot speech pattern. Another member of the Laos Underground, I feel. It is people like Deborah who change the world, one drop at a time in life's pond.

So, just when I feel I have hit the wall, along has come Deborah and that very evening, as we drive up the hill through the rainforest to our little home in the bush, two emails have arrived. One is from James Grindey, informing us that the survey, though extremely late, is at last finished and assuring us that we do not need to pay the second half of the monies owed. He also tells us that he is leaving the company, having taken up a position with a company headquartered in Dacca.

James doesn't know it but Dacca is where The Road to NaLin had a sort of beginning for us. Forty years ago when Iain and I were covering the literally bloody birth of the new nation of Bangla Desh and the resultant massive refugee crisis that occurred, we promised ourselves that one day we would do something more useful than just report on events.

The second email is from Chanthy who tells us that his Dad has found a contractor who has agreed to build The Road for roughly the same amount of the funds we now have in the bank. But time is of the essence because the rains are about to set in.

'How soon do you reckon we could go?' Iain challenges me.

'The day after tomorrow,' I respond defiantly.

Two days later we are on a plane.

23

SOMETHING OUT OF THE BOX!

NaLin, indeed Laos itself, is not a straightforward place to reach. It is not like there are direct flights. Nor is it inexpensive to get there. We have been told this is not only because Laos is tucked away, landlocked, in the heart of south east Asia, but also because Lao PDR government regulations do not give landing rights to low cost airlines, while surrounding countries are awash with budget travelers.

Rather self-defeating, one would think, for a country that could benefit financially from an increase in tourism. Though of course the likely biggest increase is already noticeably coming from China, with whom Lao shares a land border. So cheap air flights are perhaps some way down the list of priorities for the government of a country whose GDP places it 135th out of 181 countries worldwide.

This and other scatter-shot thinking overflow from my hyped brain as we leave the Great Southern Land. Thank heavens for pals Gerda and Christa who have again jumped in to fill the sudden breach in the dyke that surrounds home-ownership by house-sitting for us while we are away.

The most important detail to organize is getting the monies from the bank account of The Road to NaLin Fund transferred in the cheapest, fastest and most importantly, safest way to Laos. We consider a number of options; cash, loaded credit cards, Western Union, a bank cheque and finally settle on good old-fashioned bank transfer. The only bank account in Laos we can think of transferring the money into is Chanthy's personal account. The fact that his account, which held less than $100, was to be suddenly seriously topped up to the tune of $27,000 was never a worry for us although we knew some people might query it. The fact is we trust Chanthy implicitly.

However it doesn't help that the Lao PDR is nominally a communist state and thus sits uncomfortably within the wider world's banking system. But Suzanne Brincat, the Customer Service Specialist at our bank in Murwillumbah who has watched with interest as the RNL monies have increased is unfazed by the requests we make as soon as the door to her office opens at 9.30am on a Monday. She patiently sorts through the various hiccoughs that present themselves and even phones to some higher authority to obtain the best exchange rate possible. We can't just change

Australian dollars into Lao kip. We have to first exchange our hard-begged-for Australian currency into American dollars and then eventually exchange these for Lao kip, naturally with a fee attached to each step.

Its cheaper it seems, as well as requiring no paperwork, to change water into wine. A few strokes on the computer keyboard ends up costing the Fund $70. But a few days later Chanthy's bank account holds wealth beyond the dreams of a rice farmer's son.

Within forty-eight hours of making the decision to go for it we have over-nighted in Kuala Lumpur and Luang Prabang and are on what we will come to call The Noodle Run en route from Luang Prabang to the District Centre of Muang Nam about three hours by road south of Luang Prabang.

A 10 am meeting has been arranged with the Chief Administrative Officer of the District, the Head of the Public Works Department, as well as other local officials, plus the owner of the construction company and the headmen of NaLin and the two minority villages Houayhe and Phujong.

The large bus, that makes the daily run from Luang Prabang through to Xaiyanabouri via Muang Nam would definitely be more comfortable and perhaps marginally safer, but it would not get us there in time for this crucial get together. Instead we cram into the back tray of a small Hyundai truck.

Two metal benches, facing each other, run the length of the body and metal side poles support a roof.

We automatically slip easily back into our other lifestyle and as usual prior to the trip we go with Chanthy, who met us the previous evening on our arrival with such obvious pleasure, to do a food shop-up at Phosi market. Buffalo blood sausages for his mother and fruit and vegetables for the planned basi to welcome us. Our small backpacks are bulging with documents, computer, movie and stills cameras, iPad and small gifts from Australia.

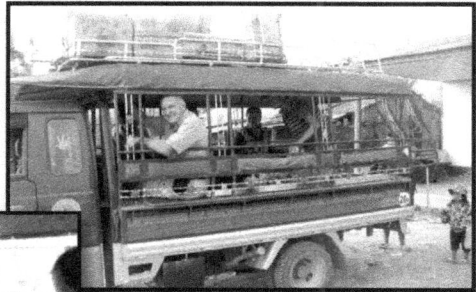

The *Noodle Run* truck for the trip to Muang Nan

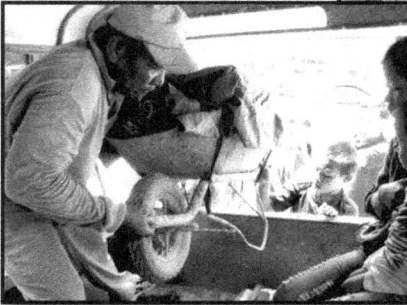

A cement-laden wheel-barrow comes aboard

We claim a position on the bench immediately behind the driver's cabin that is already overloaded with three passengers and their assorted bags, in a space designed to carry one. Other travelers cram in with the good humour and tolerance the poor invariable exhibit under such conditions. Nobody complains that almost the entire space under both side benches as well as the floor area between the benches is overflowing with the bags of one passenger. This is a woman with a great smile who herself almost disappears under even more bulging piles of large open bags that she clings to on her lap. The Noodle Lady as we come to name her, offers everyone, there are now ten of us, a piece of fruit.

By the time we bump our way out of the rutted earthen yard onto the sealed road there are twelve passengers inside, and two hanging off the back. During the three-hour journey we make frequent stops to drop off some passengers and pick up others. After the first half an hour we reach Xieng Ngeun where we turn off the tarmac road onto an unsealed road that heads southwest in the direction of Xainyanabouri. It's a road we will become uncomfortably intimate with over the following weeks.

Conversation dies away as travelers wrap their faces in scarves as protection from the billowing dust thrown up by both passing and oncoming traffic. There is a lot of government-funded work underway on this road and the number of front-end loaders, graders, and rollers we pass create a sense of urgency. Well, urgency is perhaps too strong a description. Its urgency in the laid-back Lao manner! The rains are coming. The road needs to be graded and compacted to withstand the annual tropical deluge.

A water truck passes us, spraying in the wake of a grader and we are all given a good soaking. No worries in this heat and humidity. I go into what I call my alpha state in which I can distance myself from all actual physical discomforts. The grandeur of the mountain scenery unfolds in huge dips and bends.

At each small roadside settlement we make brief stops for the Noodle Lady to exchange sometimes two, oftentimes up to five, bags of fresh noodles for much-fingered handfuls of rather well worn notes. These she quickly and expertly checks through before tucking them into a moneybag at her waist. The buyers are all women who dash out between serving customers at their *pho* or noodle stalls. It is only then we come to realise she is conducting her small business from the back of the truck. It is obviously less labour intensive and also cheaper

The Noodle Lady at work from the back of the truck

for these stall holders to buy fresh noodles made in Luang Prabang, more than likely by the Noodle Lady's family, than it would be for them to make their own.

Layered with gritty dust, our minds joggled by a sudden change of climate from the pleasant autumnal coolness of home to ferocious pre-monsoonal heat, a lack of proper sleep and the four-hour time difference with Australia's east coast, we pull into the Muang Nan market place. Here we are warmly greeted by Chanthy's Dad, Thongkhan and Uncle, Souvan Fongsamou and NaLin headman Dith Chanthamalai as well as those we have come to recognize as the hard core of NaLin's movers and shakers.

There are around three hundred people resident in NaLin but these are the faces and voices we have come to recognize and know best; because these are the ones who stand up to be counted. As in every community worldwide there are the majority of folk, those who stand back and let things happen to them and there are the leaders, the ones who take responsibility. It is not necessary to speak or understand the language to work out who's who.

They are pleased to see us and us to be with them. There is an atmosphere of confident camaraderie. Together we're going to get the job done. It's a good feeling.

In a chattering throng we cross the road and walk up to the office of Vijit Sisaiphong, Head of the Department of Public Works and Transportation. It is just over nine months since we first met Mr.Vijit. On that occasion he had surprised us by asking what we wanted to get out of building The Road to NaLin. We had told him then that all we wanted was to see a smile on the faces of the villagers of NaLin. We have no inkling, as we meet again that what we are going to be asked today will come as even more of a surprise, not to say shock.

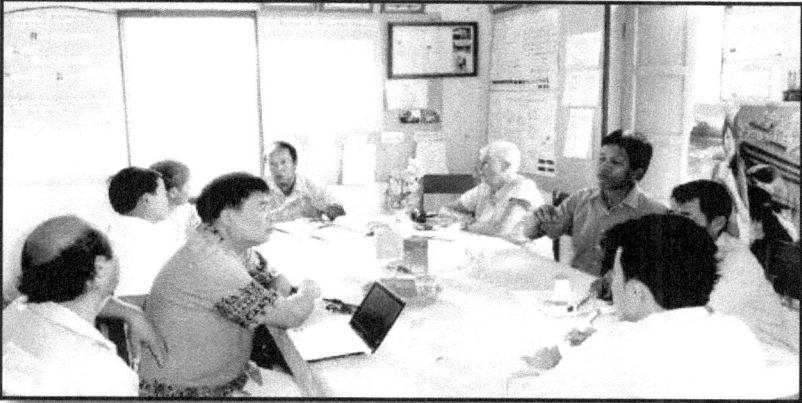

Another meeting with Mr. Vijit Sisaipon of the Public Works Department as well as some other government heavyweights

The small, simply furnished room is packed with people. More chairs are conjured up and crowded in around the long table adorned with the inevitable vase decorated with Chinese calligraphy and stuffed with plastic flowers. On the wall, surrounded by official paperwork, hangs a large Beer Lao calendar enhanced by a three-quarter-length portrait of a demurely enticing Lao beauty in national dress. All these lift disconsolately in the limpid draft raised by a slowly turning ceiling fan. The heat, oh the heat!

We shake hands with Mr. Vijit who introduces us to Mr. Thone Siumphone, Chief Administration Officer of Nan District and Mr. Khamphou Thongkhamaphone Inspector of Roads as well as Mr. Bounpheng Vannasouk who is Head of the Development Group at Khoktum village, a short distance away from the District Centre of Muang Nam. We gather from how this is done that these are people of significant importance in the game we are now playing.

I give their names out of respect to them, but also to illustrate how much there is with which the two of us have to mentally grapple. Further along the table is Mr. Pimphone, younger brother of the owner of the Khamluanglat construction company, Mr. Phali. It is explained that Mr. Phali is unable to attend but *bo peng yang,* no worries, Mr.Pimphone is his brother's right hand man. He is the works manager and foreman who will be overseeing the building of The Road to NaLin. Most importantly he can sign all legal documents in place of his brother.

There is the usual slight hesitancy that exists worldwide between those who are government employees and those who are in private business: each regarding the other with a degree of suspicion. Again I am struck by how unnecessary it is to speak or understand the actual language to be able to pick up the tenor and nuance of the conversation. All those representing the villages mill around the table, coming and going from chairs, or stand outside on the top step dragging on cigarettes.

In the hurried preparations for departure from Australia, during the flight, which is now a distant memory and in snatches of time since being in-country Iain and I have agreed that we will ask for a contract that divides the monies to be paid into three tranches; 60 million kip, about A$ 8000, 80 million kip, around $11,000 and another 60 million kip. All up around $27,000. We decided this last 60 million would not be paid until The Road is finally completed.

We have emailed the Australian Ambassador to Laos, Lynda Worthaisong, who we'd met in mid-2012, to ask her if she can arrange for a letter to be written on officially-headed paper saying we represent a group of private donors in Australia and stating how the monies for the building of the Road to NaLin will be paid in three hits. We show Vijit and the men around the table the emailed version of the Ambassador's letter and let them know the hard copy will be coming shortly.

It is embarrassing to admit we appear to have unconsciously imbibed Western fears that wily Orientals will rip us off if at all possible. As if wily Occidentals wouldn't do just the same given half a chance! Though in mitigation I would like to say this fear is greatly enlarged because we are so conscious of being responsible for getting the best deal possible for other people's monies.

This is part of our mind-set coming into this meeting. The mind-set of the Government of the Lao People's Democratic Republic, just about to be revealed, turns out to be something quite different, something totally unexpected and something totally out of the box!

The meeting, while not exactly called to order, gets underway and there is immediately a feeling that something needs to be explained to us first, before matters can go any further. We can sense Chanthy's unease so we ask him, 'What's up?'

He swallows and says, 'Actually,' this is a word he has come to use as a pause while gathering his language thoughts together, 'Actually Mr. Vijat and

Mr.Thone would like DearTrishDearIain to sign a paper to promise that DearTrishDearIain do not want to also build a Christian building. A church.'

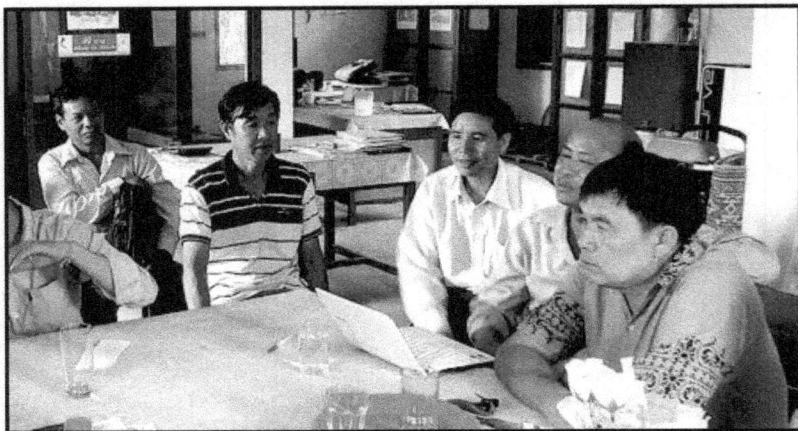

Thone Siumphone (at right) asks if we want to build a church

A church! We gawp. Perhaps its that instant gawp of amazement and laugh that persuades all of them of the truth of our response.

'No church,' Iain assures them emphatically. 'Where do we sign.' Everybody smiles. There is audible relief. Here we are two naïve muddle-headed foreigners whose first-up worry is, in a very Western way, about dollars and cents when the greatest anxiety of the locals is that we may have a hidden agenda and want to build a church.

Right. Okay. We sign. And the government people sign. The papers and the copies of copies of these papers all get the imprimatur of the Hammer and Sickle Red Stamp.

All this takes time during which I go outside to grab a gasp of somewhat cooler air while looking

230

around at the surrounding mountain peaks. Here I think about the promise we made, in another life, decades ago, to our then accountant that we would never again sign any papers unless first showing them to him. Yeah. Well. He's in a parallel universe

This initial paper signing releases a pent-up dam. The next two hours are filled with more paper signing than I will most likely do for the rest of my life. It appears that payment in three tranches is quite acceptable. In fact Mr.Pimphone seems almost disinterested in how the monies will be paid.

But not so the Government people. Fortunately for us, most fortunately as matters turn out, Mr.Khamphou is a stickler for detail. He lists ALL six of the culverts for NaLin village to be built and WHERE. He writes in the SPECIFICS about the side drainage. He puts down the EXACT distances involved. And he lists what, of all this, must be completed before the second payment will be paid. Also the third.

He assures us that he will personally come out and inspect the work. He tells us on what dates these inspections will be made. In other words he behaves professionally. All of this is typed up on manual typewriters by the two female secretarial staff and seemingly endless copies are forced from an aging copying machine and signed and re-signed and stamped and re-stamped.

Throughout all this Chanthy translates and becomes the man to whom all others now defer. He, after all, is the man with the dual language skills, apart from which, it is also his bank account that holds the monies! At one point I catch a glimpse of Chanthy's Dad looking at his son with respect and a touch of parental pride. Justifiable I think, with a catch in my throat. I imagine how I would feel if he was my own son or daughter and I was a rice farmer whose child was making a brave attempt to break the demeaning shackles of poverty.

Not once, not once during any of these or subsequent events does Chanthy ever display any sign of the hubris to which he would be somewhat entitled and which a lesser soul would surely exhibit. It is a mark of the man he has become or more than likely always was.

The ceiling fan groans on. Is it my imagination or does even the Lao calendar beauty wilt slightly? Finally it is all done, for now at least. As a sign of good faith we offer to transfer the first tranche of monies into Mr. Phali's account. There's a deal of polite joshing when it turns out that Mr. Pimphone doesn't know the bank account number. Using the ubiquitous mobile phone he rings his brother. The account number is written on a scrap of paper and Mr. Pimphone invites us all to a celebratory lunch at the local street corner café.

With Chanthy we go off to the Banque Pour Le Commerce Exterieur Lao Public, where in the sudden, sharp chill of air-conditioning, the manager, teller and armed security chap are all slurping up bowls of *pho*. They stop long enough for the manager to reprimand Iain for taking a photograph of Chanthy casually making a transfer of some $8,000 to the road-builder's bank account.

Before lunch we pay another visit, this one to the worksite where the company's heavy machinery is parked. Noting that the roller is somewhat decrepit we are assured by Mr. Pimphone that although it is not

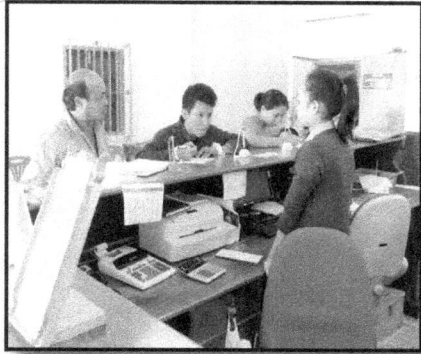

Chanthy makes the first payment

working at present, a spare part is being brought from Thailand.

The disabled roller: A new part is on its way... or so we are told

This information gives us a slight pause but we are unwilling to let such a little matter deflate our by now over the top excitement that the Road to NaLin is about to happen.

Under a huge hanging wild bee's hive that serves as décor for the café and which is fortunately

233

unoccupied, we eat the first of what over the coming weeks will be many, many bowls of *pho pak* vegetarian soup. All the others of course eat buffalo meat soup and leave their veggies: in hindsight probably a wise choice. As the meal comes to an end there's a lot of tooth picking and sucking and the owner of the café goes back to squat on his knees in an intricately carved and seemingly, to me, uncomfortably hard chair to watch his daily diet of tragic TV soaps beamed in from Thailand. These are always chockablock with ghosts and love entanglements that invariable end badly.

Pimphone leaves us to go round up his drivers, operators and roustabouts, saying he will see us in NaLin that afternoon. We clamber into the back of the village headman's Hyundai for the ride into the place that's become our second home, to witness the Road to NaLin being built. The emotions are surreal. It is extremely difficult to believe that after two and a half years it is really happening.

24

THE WORK BEGINS

We are met by Chanthy's mother, Buachan Phonemanee, holding in her arms the now seven-month-old Mr. Sydney. I restrain my natural instinct to give him a big cuddle because I know with my pale hair and blue eyes I am an unusual and therefore frightening spectre. A *falang*. A spirit person. A *phii*. Instead I content myself with smiling, not too broadly, at him from a non-threatening distance. Happily I find he is not too repulsed or nervous and by leaving him to work me out at his own speed I am rewarded over the coming days by being able to sit with him on my lap as long as Mum or Grandma are in view.

Pimphone is true to his word and come mid-afternoon, his convoy of machines and trucks roll into the village and the fun begins. There is an excavator, whose arm is manipulated by a Mr. Ken

235

and a grader smoothly driven by a Mr. Done. Both machines are a bright yellow. They are followed by two much-used and battered ten-tonne tipper-trucks one driven by Mr.Phuang and the other one by Mr. Saeng. The back tyre-flaps on Saeng's truck carry the famous monochrome graphic of the Argentinean Marxist revolutionary, Che Gueverra. I ask Chanthy if he recognizes the portrait. He doesn't. There is also a roustabout, another Mr. Ken, who charges about in a ute like a blowfly on a carcass. Orchestrating all this is Pimphone.

But as we'd already been told...no roller.

Work begins: On the road, in the village and at the quarry

No input from us is needed to arrange for soil and rock for the project. It is all to be excavated from a hillside plot of land about a kilometer outside of NaLin village. Mr. Phar Vilaisone who owns this land says he has always wanted to enlarge a flat space there, as he and his family may one day want to build a dwelling on it.

In another sign of spontaneous generosity and community-mindedness an old, disused one-room attap hut, raised on stilts, has been made available by the same man as a campsite and worksite for the men.

Work begins immediately. Ducks, chickens, turkeys and dogs scatter to safety and by the time the villagers begin to return in the late afternoon, from working in their paddy fields, they find their road has become a busy worksite. Many, many loads of topping have already been tipped and spread to fill in, raise, round off and smooth out the rutted track. They make their way around and over the piles of earth and past the machines with looks of pleasure and interest.

I experience something of a high and forgetting the blow-to-the brain heat, clamber up into the cabin of the Che-adorned truck. Chanthy,

Villagers watch the work get under way

no-doubt anxious for my safety, gets up behind me as we set off for the excavation site.

Through Chanthy I ask the driver, Saeng whether he was interested in trucks when he was a young boy. This is how Chanthy translated his answer:

'Yes. Since I was a very small boy I have been attracted to trucks and wanted to drive them. It was my childhood dream. And now I am living my dream.'

I know its sounds schmaltzy; 'I am living my dream.' But it is what he says and judging by the look on his face, I believe him. Even though the job entails bush camping and sleeping rough and the pay is only the equivalent of $10 a day. In a country where most people manage to just scrape by on around $2 to $3 a day, he is relatively well off. No Unions of course, so no one to speak up for you if your employer 'forgets' to pay you. No holiday loadings, or even holiday pay. No workplace safety regulations, superannuation payments, long service or even sickness benefits. It would be impossible to explain the concept of maternity/paternity leave.

I have heard how the Australian and other Western Governments have tied their Aid Funding to workplace conditions, not only in Laos but in many other even poorer economies. International labour regulations of course make this a necessity. In Laos we know of teachers in government schools and colleges who have not been paid for upwards of two months. There are other stories of the same happening to police officers and immigration officials. Though I doubt the Prime Minister ever misses out on his pay packet. What to do?

Suddenly the combination of heat, humidity, constant action and excessive excitement stuns me, literally and I lie down in a corner of the main room of Chanthy's parent's home on a thin blanket spread out on the linoleum that covers the cement floor and fall into a pit of deep slumber.

When I crawl back to consciousness an hour or so later, the light is no longer so harsh, though the heat remains and I become aware that Iain has flaked out beside me and is still deep asleep. At the other end of the room Mr. Phou Simaneevong, the elderly cousin/uncle who shares the family's main room, is squatting on his unbelievably thin haunches watching through the open doorway as a section of The Road passing through the village begins to take shape.

The work camp on the edge of the village

Iain stirs and we pull our-selves together enough to walk the changed road to the edge of the village where, in the now fast failing light, Pimphone and his men, having had a wash up in the river are beginning to make preparations for the evening meal.

239

Iain asks if he can film them. They have set up a campfire and a minute or so after we arrive, Headman Mr. Dith walks in carrying a large duck by its wings. Dinner.

We leave them to it and go off for our own river wash-up. Its far from refreshing because the trickle of last year's rainwater still coming down from the mountains is warm, moves sluggishly and hardly comes up to our knees. We need the rains, but please not before the roller!

Back in the house the preparations for the welcome basi are well underway. This time the celebration is a small, intimate encounter. Brother Jai is back from the rice paddies and is helping his wife Binh Chanthabundith finely chop buffalo meat to prepare the *laap* they all enjoy most. Knowing that Iain and I are not big on buffalo Jai has taken time out of his physically demanding workday to catch a few small bone-filled fish from his Uncle Souvan's small dam to feed the two of us.

Sydney, freshly bathed at the water pump out back, is being passed around between everyone. He is an affable baby and goes easily from lap to lap. Grandpa Thongkhan is obviously delighted at having a grandchild.

Mr. Thongdy arrives to officiate at the basi. This former monk is even older than Iain, a fact in which he revels. No visit to NaLin is complete without Thongdy comparing ages with Iain and making sure we understand that he has half a decade on him. Thongdy who is invariably neatly turned out, has one of those faces that always seems to show happiness or contentment.

I have come prepared with special scarves, ones my sister bought while she was living in Italy. I like the concept of including her in this ceremony. The family all nods approvingly as we drape these left to right from over our shoulder across our heart as a sign of respect. The ceremony begins.

The moment the ceremony is completed, Sydney, who has somehow realized this is a special occasion and has remained silently attentive throughout, now goes for broke with the goodies; attempting to stuff everything, puffed wheat, lollies still in their wrappings, into his mouth and is gently restrained by his Granddad.

The ceremonial platter and the special floor cloth are removed and with no further ado the food comes out in bowls from the kitchen and is set on the floor. Sticky rice is balled up in one hand, dipped into sauce and used as a base for gathering up meat and veggies from other dishes. The dish of small fried fish, a bit like sardines, is placed between Iain and myself. No fuss. It all happens seamlessly with tremendous grace amid plenty of happy chatter. We feel blessed to have been accepted as members of this family.

As soon as the dishes are empty they are cleared away and our thin mattresses are rolled out from the wall where they are piled up during the day. The mosquito net is hung and we clamber inside our sleeping space. Chanthy's mattress is unrolled a slight distance away, also shrouded by a net. Neighbours wander in and out for a short while longer but by 8.30pm the front door is shut. Mum and Dad, Jai, Binh and Mr. Sydney go upstairs. Mr. Phou has been in his curtained 'room' long since. There is silence.

But there is still light, because the overhead fluorescent is left on, to inhibit night-spirits and as I lie on my side in my sarong and by this light, I count the sacks of rice that are piled at this end of the room: the end product of so much hard work. There are over a hundred, worth about $2 each in the market. But sold only in situations of dire need. This is the staple survival food for the family and must last them a year. Above them, hanging from the rafters are many clusters of full garlic heads. Also never sold unless financial need demands.

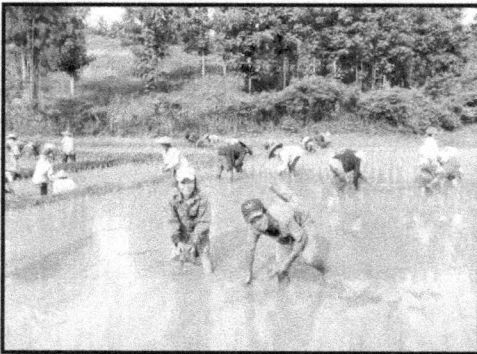

Chanthy's parents:
Buachan and
ThongKhan

Thongkhan and Buachan have worked 70-hour weeks for a whole year in order to reach just this basic level of economic stability for their family.

25

MARRIAGE ARRANGMENTS

Early to bed and early to rise is the way of life in NaLin. The first cockerels begin to crow a little before 5am. Not long after that Jai leaves for his long day of work in the fields. He is clearing land, rented from another villager, on which he plans to plant hops. This is a new crop for local farmers. A crop they can sell, through middlemen, to the Beer Lao Company. It is a little risky because, unlike rice, you can't eat hops.

But Jai is of the next generation and therefore more willing to take chances and grab opportunities. He wants to do more than live hand to mouth. He has plans. He wants to put cash money aside for Sydney's future education. So he works even more hours than his Mother and Father; early mornings preparing his rented land for hops and the remaining hours of sunlight in either his own family's rice paddy or the fields of his wife's family.

When a Lao man marries he must pay a bride

price, a dowry. It is the reverse of what is the custom in India for example. His family must also pay for the wedding party. Jai's marriage and wedding cost his Mum and Dad the totally over the top huge amount of 33 million kip. That's $4500; a sum they borrowed from a relative and that could take a very long time to pay back.

If I write that despite all this they got a good deal, you might flinch, especially if you are a woman. But, taking on board that's how society works in Laos, it is a fact. His wife Binh, although young, seems to be a terrific mother, a solid worker and to top it all she has a warm and pleasantly caring disposition. There are no hiding true characteristics when living as up close and personal as one does in a small village home.

Once married, a Lao man leaves his home and moves in to live with and care for his wife's parents. Jai and Binh have already made a generational break with some of these traditions by living part of the week with his family and part with hers and by Jai working in his parents-in-law rice farm as well as that of his own parents: all that on top of the new venture into hops.

This is large workload even for a man of 24, but though he may not be aware of the actual statistics, Jai would know just by looking around him at the other men in his village, that he's already well past a third of the way through his expected life span. He doesn't need statistics to tell him he needs to get into it before life pitches him a curve ball. Earlier this year he spent time in hospital with an undiagnosed stomach complaint. Giardia, Japanese encephalitis, dengue fever, are all endemic and any of them, if untreated, can be deadly.

Through the veil of the mosquito net I see Binh give her husband a small leaf-wrapped packet of sticky rice to sustain him through the long workday and Jai nuzzle his son before unhooking his sharp *parang* from the wall by the door and heading on out. Binh joins her mother-in-law who is already crouching over the open hearth in the tiny dark workspace off the back of the main room that does duty as the family kitchen.

Chanthy has rolled up his mat and left the house, so we roll ours, also folding and storing the mosquito net, because we know from experience that he will shortly return with the inevitable two eggs to be fried for each of us. While we are eating these eggs and answering Chanthy's gentle inquiries as to how we have slept, we hear the rumble of the loaded trucks followed by the grader.

But before we can follow them, we first chat to Sengchan Sitanong, a next-door neighbour who has wandered in through the door as if it's the most natural thing in the world to do. Here it obviously is. He has come in from his small woodworking workshop at the back of his house and has the bottom of his trousers rolled up so it is impossible not to notice and therefore comment on his seriously scarred lower leg. Having seen inside his very basic workshop we both assume the damage was an industrial accident. But no.

'It's a bullet-wound' Sengchan explains. 'The

bullet went in here,' he touches the leg to the side of the shin bone 'and came out here,' he massages the destroyed calf muscle. 'They wanted to take it all away. But I said no.'

'Where were you?' Iain asks.

'Xiengkhuang.'

Xiengkhuang Province, where we had visited with Chanthy, experienced the worst and heaviest of the fighting and air bombardment during the Vietnam War.

'The Plain of Jars', Iain comments. 'Were you in the Pathet Lao?'

Sengchan nods and asks, 'Were you in the war too?'

'Not really.' Iain hesitates. 'I was a journalist. I reported on the war in Vietnam, for television.'

Sengchan speaks into the middle distance. 'Real war is very different from how it looks on television.'

Hitching a lift in one of the returning trucks out to the temporary quarry we are astonished to see that the entire semi-circular rim is encrusted with small children. The primary school, we are told, has given them all time off to enjoy the miracle that is The Road. Hunkered down on their haunches they wave and clap as the frontend loader grabs out another big scoop of earth and rock and gravel and loads it into the back tray of a truck. I wonder how many small lads watching this day's proceedings will dream of one day driving such equipment and how many of them will 'live their dream.' More pebbles in the pond of life.

By nine o'clock we are back in the village where unexpectedly we are introduced to Mr. Phali Khamluanglat, the owner of the eponymous construction company. He has a young lad of perhaps five with him and it is obvious that this is his son. From Chanthy we have learnt that not only does Phali have a wife and family in Vientiane, but a second wife and a second family in Muang Nan. Over the previous days, we have discovered Phali has somewhat more than that. He has five, if we can believe it, second wives and what is more he has children with them all. A busy man.

As the days pass and the mornings heat up with more topping being dumped and spread and graded and more videoing being done, it becomes obvious the need for the roller is becoming imperative. Pimphone insists that the replacement part for the roller is definitely on its way from Thailand and assures us that time waiting for the roller will not be wasted, because the crew can spend the next few days installing the six culvert drains on the approach and exit roads to the village.

These big concrete culverts, that have been offloaded at their campsite, will require ditches to be dug across The Road and a bed of concrete to be poured in which they will sit so as to ensure water running in from higher levels on one side of The Road can flow through the drains to lower levels on the other side and eventually into the nearby river.

Installing the culvert drains

As there is nothing we can physically do ourselves to build The Road any faster we decide to take the taxi-truck back up to Luang Prabang where we can at least catch our breath, download the video and stills into the comparative safety of our computers and be in touch with family and friends, most of whom, because of the more or less instantaneous manner of our departure, don't even know we have left.

248

But being in Luang Prabang means we will not be able to get any shots of the culverts going in, so I leave my camera, with a fully charged battery, with Chanthy's father Thongkhan, asking him to keep taking shots of the building of the culverts until the battery goes flat. Chanthy explains this to his Dad and adds my suggestion to take 'natural shots, nothing posed.' I need not have been so condescending. Thongkhan took to photography as if to the manner born.

As we are leaving Muang Nam in the taxi-truck Chanthy points out to us the high school he had attended for six years. He had told us previously how he had boarded in the township with a friend of his father, paying for his keep by cooking and cleaning for the family. Every weekend he walked a thirty kilometer round trip, over two small mountains in order to work on his parent's farm: home on Friday afternoon back to Muang Nan on Sunday afternoon.

Now we can see, rather than just hear about this journey, it of course becomes far more real. What Chanthy hadn't told us before, but did so now, was that the family treated him, in our terms, like a skivvy. Not only was he expected to cook and clean but also to collect firewood from the forest. 'I was very frightened,' Chanthy shudders slightly, 'of the spirits.'

I am starting to understand this fear of spirits a little better because I now knew that it is very usual in Laos for bodies of the dead to be laid to rest in unmarked shallow graves among the trees that cloak almost all of the country. Very few families can afford the far preferred method of corporeal incineration in a wat, followed by a scattering of the ashes in the river. Naturally it is thought that the spirits of these abandoned bodies hang about and perform unspeakable acts on those who stray into their domain. Being compelled to collect forest wood for cooking among these spirits would have been a terrifying task for a particularly imaginative young boy.

'By my last year at high school I told my parents I couldn't live like this anymore,' Chanthy admits. 'But my Mother said, 'Chanthy you have to stay and finish your schooling.' So I did.'

'The man's two sons, who were around the same age as me, were paid by their father for what they collected, but I was never given anything and those two boys took great pleasure in this,' Chanthy told us as he pointed out the house where he stayed during those six years. 'But I think it did them no good. They both became drug addicts and their father has had to sell everything in order to buy their drugs and keep them out of prison.' Then in the closest we had ever heard Chanthy come to expressing a negative thought he adds, 'I think the Buddha is correct that doing bad things brings bad things.' After a pause, he adds, '...and doing good things brings good things.'

Up, up, up the taxi-truck strains, although not so fully laden for this return trip, to get onto the ridgeline. The dust from the road-works clogs our nostrils and hair and pores so it's a relief when we slow down at a cluster of simple wooden houses and a group of women surge forward offering bamboo shoots and wild mushrooms, the local specialties, for sale. We purchase some to take back for our Luang Prabang guesthouse family of Noi and Thiemchanh and for Chanthy to cook up for himself and his sister. Half an hour later, we drop him at his student dormitory room to be met by Bounlee, who hadn't come down to the village with us because she's been putting the final touches to her course-end presentation paper.

For us, it is the bliss of the air-conditioning in our own room at Khoumxiengthong Guest House. We wash away the dust, unpack our gear and begin sending emails.

26

LOW EBB

It was great to have clean hair and skin and to sleep between sheets, to do our morning cycle alongside the Mekong and have almond croissant for breakfast. What wimpy suburban souls we have! It was also good to be reassured the stills and movie camera were functioning properly, along with my bowel which refuses to function in the clean but primitive squat loo at the back of the Sisombuth family home.

It was also good to catch up with Khamchanh Bounprasird our novice, or now more accurately ex-novice, friend, whom we had met at the same time as we had met Chanthy, two and a half years ago. Though it was a somewhat disconcerting to sit at dinner with him wearing jeans and tee-shirt, the first time we had seen him out of his orange robes, talking about his new, bicycle, while showing us a new digital camera.

Khamchanh, or as he now prefers, Chanh, has

252

been befriended by a middle aged American woman, who has provided for these gifts and who is funding the next part of his education at a private college in Vientiane.

'I have a passport now,' he takes the document from his new briefcase, 'and I am going to meet up with my American mum in Singapore.' Happily he appears to be taking all of these enormous life changes in his stride.

But we know this is not what we are here for or where we should be. Especially when the message comes through from Thongkhan that all the culverts are now in place, but unfortunately the roller part that arrived from Bangkok turned out to be the wrong part and the man has been re-dispatched to Bangkok to bring back the correct one. So Pimphone is now planning to pull all the road building machinery out of NaLin.

Khamphou has made an inspection of the work that has been done and wishes to discuss payment of the second tranch of monies.

We stock up on canned sardines, pay another visit to Phosi market and are greeted with warm smiles by the Noodle Lady whose bags again already overflow from under the seats as well as filling the space between everyone's knees. The row of small but intense bruises on my hips and spine twinge uncomfortably as we settle in for the run.

This time when we stop for some bamboo shoots from the same roadside sellers we bought from on the way up we also change a worrisomely soft tyre. In the time that takes we check out a mobile toys and trinkets shop.

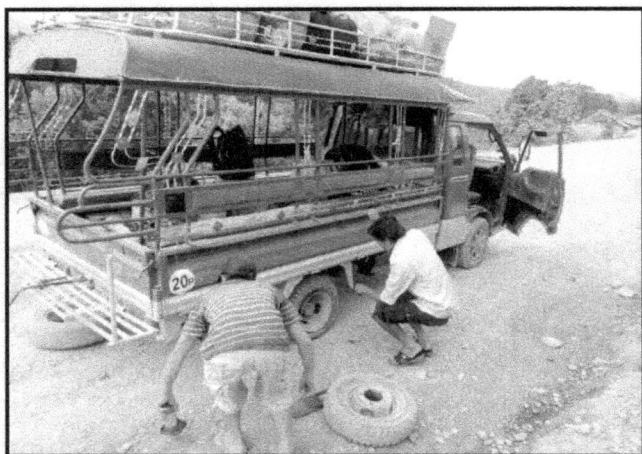

We stop to change a flat tyre

A travelling salesman has set up his store of garishly attractive, cheap products on a tarpaulin at the dusty edge of the road. To attract attention to his presence he has loudly distorted music pouring from a speaker in the back of his wagon that obviously serves double duty as his sleep space.

We purchase a soft rubber ball for Sydney and try to engage in a casual chat with the chain-smoking vendor, who is recognizably Chinese. He tells us 'I have been traveling the back roads of Laos for eight years. I stop in any place that has no shops. I bring what they want.'

The tyre replaced, we take to the road once more again impressed by the amount of roadwork that is underway and the number of rollers, many of which seem to be idle. 'Perhaps we could 'borrow' one of them I suggest, only half-jokingly.

As before we make frequent stops for the Noodle Lady to conduct her business from the back of the truck. By journey's end she has sold her stock and stays on the truck for the return trip to Luang Prabang.

Headman Dith and Chanthy's Dad, Thongkhan, again meet us in Muang Nan. But this time their greeting is somewhat subdued. On our previous visit there had been a conversation about the possibility of rebuilding and at the same time enlarging the small dam on the Sisombuth farmlet that had deteriorated over many storms and rainy seasons. So before heading off to NaLin, we load up the truck tray with ten bags of cement and a dozen or so metal reinforcing rods.

The cost is only $80 for which we make a personal contribution towards the dam. On the drive out to the village a pleased Thongkhan explains that on the day of the next full moon, the day of the month when all villagers pitch in to help anyone who requires extra hands, they would begin the task of getting the enlargement to the dam underway. The hope is that bigger water storage facilities will make it possible for the Sisombuth's farm to produce two rice crops a year, as happens in many other parts of the country. The longed for all-seasons-road will make it possible to get this extra crop to market.

Seated on the floor of the Sisombuth house are Headman Dith and Thongkhan, Government Road Inspector Khamphou, with his sheaf of much-signed paperwork and construction overseer Pimphone alongside Chanthy and us. The humid heat is as usual, intense. From the outset it is apparent that Khamphou is anxious. He estimates that the job is 80% complete and tells us that Pimphone would like to be paid a further 100 million kip, around $12,000, instead of the agreed second tranche payment of 80 million kip. Khamphou spreads papers across the thin matting and points to figures and signatures.

We insist that the work is not 80% complete and that we will pay only 80 million kip

Before he can continue, Iain begins to query him about what has and has not been done. Yes the culverts are in place, along with tonnes and tonnes of topsoil that has been spread and graded. But where is the roller? It is the crucial element in the work. Without it all the work already done, could be lost. Pimphone should not expect any more than the agreed and signed for second payment when there is not even any sign of this crucial roller and he's preparing to pull all of the rest of the equipment out. Iain insists on paying only the amount of the second tranche, namely 80 million kip, leaving 60 million kip held back in reserve until the job is done.

Headman Dith gets up to walk around outside and I come to understand he is a person who does not like any degree of expressed dissension. Khamphou looks like he would dearly love to join him but realizes he can't because he's the man with the lists of dates and monies and all the signed papers. Thongkhan by contrast sits on through the disagreements with the air of a man determined to be there at the end. Figures, dates and options are tossed to and fro. Iain hangs tough, while remaining unfailingly polite.

The roller. Talk always returns to the phantom roller. When will the vitally necessary part arrive? Can we be certain it will be the right part this time? Is it not possible to hire another roller from another company?

Moving outside, I sit in the shade of the army veteran's house beside his wife who is cutting and then splitting bamboo with a ferociously sharp knife. She does this so automatically she can simultaneously carry on a conversation with the women who come and go from beside her on the bench. The ducks and chickens peck around us for un-seeable scraps.

I count the strips she binds together into bundles of fifty strips. Chanthy has explained these strips are used as ties to hold together bamboo poles that will form a fence they are building around a small vegetable plot to keep out the rats. He has also told me that a bunch of ties sells in the market for the equivalent of seventeen cents. To make roughly $3.00 in a day, she has to cut almost 1000 strips, or 20 bundles. Even if she could do them at breakneck speed, I don't need to do the math to know its monotonous work for very little reward and all part of the intricately throttling pattern of poverty.

The men come out of the Sisombuth's house and I join them to walk back over The Road. An agreement has been struck. The previously agreed to second payment will be paid, with none of the asked-for extras, but Pimphone will pull out his men and machines, which can of course earn money working elsewhere and will return only when the roller is in working order.

On the edge of the village the equipment is already lined up in convoy ready to leave. Lightning flashes in the surrounding mountains, the sky suddenly darkens

The heavy equipment starts to rollout

with thunderheads and as if on cue rain begins to fall.

The onset of the wet season nears as rain begins to fall

We are a forlorn, bedraggled and damply defeated looking team as we walk back over The Road whose un-compacted surface we know, if these rains continue and become even more heavy, will all too rapidly deteriorate.

Headman Dith looks downcast. Iain and I feel pretty low. The villagers, returning now from their day's fieldwork have expressions of defeat. Chanthy is uncharacteristically quiet. Only Thongkhan appears unperturbed. He is nothing if not a survivor.

One of the great things about small children is that their total self-centeredness does not make allowances for what may be happening in the adult world. So we play ball with a happy Sydney while his evening bathing rituals are underway and dinner is made.

Thongkhan examines the can of sardines we have brought to eat and asks if he can use the ring-pull to open it. His obvious pleasure in this simple new experience, as well as in tasting a sardine, lifts our spirits and we make a mental note to bring him some cans of sardines from Luang Prabang in a few days time.

Lying sleepless under the mosquito net that night I have what seems like a brainwave. But I can't risk waking the household by sharing it with Iain so I have to keep it to myself until dawn. By the time the chorus of chooks heralds the start of a new day I have decided to keep the thought to myself until we are on our own.

The road journey back up to Luang Prabang is enlivened by the arrival of a novice who, at one of the passenger pickup stops, seems to levitate himself sideways into the back of the taxi-truck. In an unusually open display of interest for a novice, he inquires through Chanthy what we foreigners are up to in outback Laos and asks if we will be coming back down for *Boun Bung Fai*, The Rocket Festival. He assures us that he will be there. He is looking forward to it.

Odd, I think, that a Buddhist novice should be excited at the prospect of this animist festival, even though I know this specifically Lao occasion is a much loved event on the annual festival calendar.

During *Boun Bung Fai* giant rockets are fired from bamboo platforms into the sky, as a petition to the gods I imagine, in the hope of bringing on the rain. This year's festival is set for the coming weekend of the 23rd/24th of May. Our contract with the Khamluanglat Road Building Company expires on Saturday 25th. It is all coming down to the wire: Roller. Rocket Festival. Rain. Hopefully in that order.

After the novice has dismounted to visit, he tells us, friends at another wat, we travel on through the gritty dust up onto the ridgeline. This is the road we first travelled over a year ago, at that time in the heavy rains and where we had witnessed first-hand the entrepreneurial nouse of the Lao. At that time all along the steep, high, red banks of mud that reared up from each side of the then muddy track, scores of young men were hunkered down on their haunches, seemingly waiting.

We had asked Chanthy, 'What are these men waiting for?'

'They are waiting for our vehicle or any other vehicle to get bogged down in the mud and need to be pushed. They charge for their help, perhaps as much as a dollar.' Now the road is far wider, bordered by deep drainage ditches and has a compacted surface this muscle power is no longer required. That job opportunity at least as far as this particular village is concerned, has gone into the dustbin of history.

There is just one further human drama to be witnessed. While negotiating its way through one of the tiny hamlets strung out along the road, avoiding the dogs and chooks as well as numerous children well under ten years of age who are struggling, barefoot, to carry pails of water from some distant spigot to their thatch roofed home, the taxi-truck slews to a stop just in time to avoid colliding head on with a wild haired young woman.

She races to the back of the truck and tries to clamber aboard. Her tear-streaked face is twisted with anguish. She already has a fearsome hold on the tailgate when two women seize her from behind. From their appearance and manner it is safe to assume they are her mother and sister. They violently break her hold on the vehicle and drag her backwards. She screams and holds out her arms imploringly toward all of us who sit stunned into silent immobility. The driver moves slowly forward. She breaks free and runs after us. But the other two women rush to grab her and she collapses in a sobbing heap in the dust. No one in the back of our truck makes eye contact with anyone else. In one sense its a relief when moments later, we move out of the dust onto the tarmac of the north/south highway and pick up some speed. But there is also the nagging doubt about what was pushing this young woman to such extremes of anguish and whether it was right to just drive off without offering some sort of assistance.

Back in Luang Prabang, washed and brushed to the best level we can manage, we have a meal on the riverside patio of the classy Belle Rive Hotel and I tell Iain of my brainwave.

'Florent Lavabre,' I say. 'Remember, the Frenchman who first estimated that building a road would cost $10,000 per kilometer and who runs that heavy equipment and plant sales place.'

'RMA', Iain dredges up the name of the company.

'The very one. He is certain to know someone with a roller for hire.' I try to sound extra positive. 'We can at least ask. Let's phone him.'

Iain does so and we arrange to go by Florent's office in the morning.

Our reunion is another turning point. Florent has fallen in love, like so many of his countrymen did in the last century, with Laos and has made it his home. He is interested in hearing about how our Road plans have developed. When we tell him about our problems with the roller he asks us to leave it with him and on the following day gives us the name and telephone number of a man he is sure can help us. What is more the man, a Mr. Lea and his company, Muasone Constructions, are based very near Muang Nan.

We steal Chanthy away from his work at Kopnoi to visit the bank

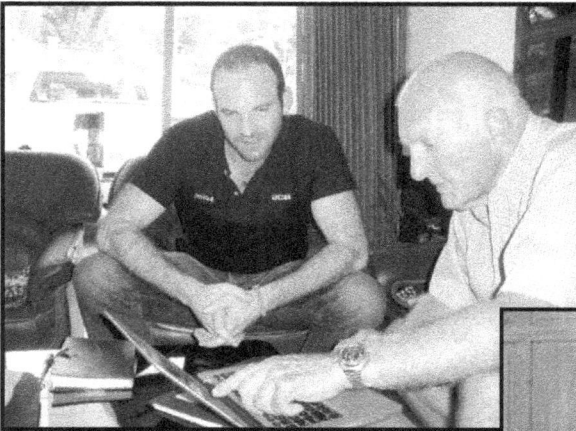

Florent Lavabre suggests a new contractor with a working roller and Chanthy lines him up to complete the work on The Road To NaLin

in order to transfer the second tranche of monies into Mr. Phali's account and in the privacy of the top floor of a local coffee shop, we break the good news about the possibility of getting another roller to finish the work. Chanthy's relief is obvious. He has already heard from his father that morning, asking what DearIainDearTrish plan to do and saying how anxious the villagers are about their Road.

Iain explains that first we, which means Chanthy, have to call Mr. Lea, owner of the Muasone Construction Company and ask him if he has a functioning roller available to start work on Sunday, which would be the day after the expiration of the contract with Pimphone's company. Today is Wednesday. If he does have one, then Chanthy needs to explain the background to our need and finally ask him about the cost.

'It is most important,' Iain tells Chanthy, 'that Mr. Lea understands that because of our contract with Pimphone he must keep this inquiry confidential.'

'We need to keep all this very close to our chest.' Iain says. '

Chanthy's eyes sparkle at this new aphorism, especially when Iain explains that it comes from the world of card games.

'Fingers crossed,' Iain says as he gives Chanthy the telephone number. This requires more explanations and brings about more happiness on Chanthy's part. He loves learning new words and sayings.

Mr. Lea answers the phone himself. Without hesitation Chanthy, this twenty-two year-old rice farmer's son, the first of his generation to break the bonds, confidently presents his problem and asks his questions.

'Yes,' Mr. Lea responds, he has a roller. It is presently working on the Lao/Thai financed dam that is being built on the Mekong River a little more than a half-day's drive from Muang Nan. But it could be brought back up to the district to do a small job. Yes, he knows where NaLin is and knows the section of the road we're talking about. He'll go out there this afternoon and without telling anyone why he is there he will have a look at what is needed. He's pretty sure he can complete the job over a couple of days.

Chanthy explains that our contract with the Khamluanglat Road Building Company expires on Saturday night and Mr. Lea responds that, yes he could step immediately into the breach on Sunday. But he knows of Mr. Phali and his company and he definitely does not want to step on any toes.

Finally Chanthy asks Mr. Lea how much the work will cost. When he tells him the price, Chanthy raises his thumb to us in the universal OK sign. After reminding Mr. Lea again of the need for confidentiality and arranging to call him again on Thursday, once we have completed yet another meeting in Muang Nan with the government transport officials as well as with Pimphone, Chanthy rings off.

The cost of the work Mr. Lea has quoted is just

on half what we have agreed to pay Mr. Phali in the final tranche. We will have more than enough money to complete the job. We sit there like a trio of Cheshire Cats, not something I try explaining to Chanthy. We have a celebratory hot chocolate and agree to travel back down to NaLin the following morning, after of course first doing a shop up at Phosi market.

As we part company, for the evening, we remind Chanthy that not even his Dad or Headman Dith or anyone else in NaLin must get wind of what's afoot. 'This is not being mean Chanthy,' Iain explains. 'But in order to play our strongest hand we need this to be a bolt from the blue.'

'We need to keep the joker up our sleeve,' I add my cliché to the pile.

Having laughingly deciphered the language, Chanthy beams with pleasure and even seems to relish the keeping of the secret.

'No worries,' he says holding up his thumb.

'Bo pen nyang,' we agree.

27

ROCKET FESTIVAL and ROLLER!

The following morning's taxi-truck Noodle Run journey down to Muang Nan is so tightly over-packed that even before we leave town Iain is muttering promises to us and himself; 'Never again. It is too dangerous. We're pushing our luck. We'll travel back by bus,' which will be only minimally safer. 'Enough already.'

Perhaps the extra crowd crammed aboard is due to this being the opening night of the two-day Rocket Festival in the district centre of Muang Nan.

I go into my alpha-state and so hardly notice and am therefore unperturbed by the large wheelbarrow and several heavy whetting stones that are loaded on board at some stage. The various bruises I seem to have picked up will probably take weeks to fade, but I glide through the gritty clouds of road dust just happy in the knowledge that at last we will have a roller and with this we can finish The Road. Please, I silently beg the rain gods, hold off for three more

267

days.

Once again we are met at Muang Nam by Thongkhan and Headman Dith. They look so downcast it is tempting to tell them about the roller, but we know the element of surprise at the upcoming afternoon meeting in Muang Nan with officialdom and with Pimphone, is essential. We're pretty sure that Pimphone is going to press for an extension of the contracted finish date for The Road, probably for another week or ten days. We are determined not to allow the extension.

We go first to a simple guesthouse on the main street of Muang Nan where we have booked to stay for this evening's Rocket Festivities. After a wash and brush-up we head out to eat at one of the two or three local cafes. Our choice of eating place turns out to be fortuitous because seated at a large table, surrounded by convivial underlings, is the Chief Administration Officer of Nan District, Mr. Thone, whom we had met at the initial contract-signing.

It is a pretty good bet that as Chief Administration Officer for a whole District Mr. Thone has some pretty serious Party political affiliations. I remember that at the previous meeting, when concerns were raised about building a church, it was he who brought them up.

However from his friendly manner and conversation, translated through Chanthy, it is apparent he is pleased The Road is happening and he tells us that he will be present again at the upcoming meeting; always good to have the powers-that-be on your side; at least that's how it seemed.

The screeching noise of extra chairs being dragged into position around Mr. Vijit's table is not quite enough to suffocate the unspoken tension in the atmosphere. Ms. Beer Lao maintains her calendar poise, but Pimphone can't quite maintain eye contact with us.

Mr. Vijit's opening remarks are brief. He briskly hands over to Chief Roads Inspector Khamphou, who outlines what everyone already knows about the work that has been done, the payments that have been made and concludes with the obvious fact that because the Khamluanglat Road Building Company's roller is not yet repaired we will need to allow an extension of time on the contract.

Both Iain and I shake our heads emphatically and Iain says, 'No,' politely but firmly.

'But there is no other way,' Khamphou says sadly, with a touch of embarrassment, even of regret because, after all, it is he who drew up these date-dependent contracts the company cannot now fulfill.

Village Headman Dith and Thongkhan stare into middle distance, both disconsolate. The assorted public servants leaf abstractly through sheaths of paperwork. The fan whirs and Pimphone looks like he wishes he was somewhere else, while Chief Admin Officer Thone, who I think knows we have a joker to play, looks at us inquiringly.

'When can I tell them? Chanthy asks. 'Can I tell

them now?

'Tell them,' Iain says, 'their contract runs for another fifty-eight hours. If they don't have a roller by then, the contract will expire. They have known what the dates and requirements were from the beginning. We will not be paying any more monies.'

Chanthy translates.

Pimphone is not a hard-nosed operator. In fact he appears embarrassed as he makes one last flustered bid for time. The roller, he tries assuring us, yet again, with his genial smile, will come. We will just have to wait. He is absolutely certain of that and so is surprised when again we shake our heads adamantly.

'No,' Iain insists, from a known position of strength.

Headman Dith and Chanthy's father, Thongkhan both look desolate but seriously puzzled and I am drenched with misery for them. I suddenly feel at first hand the powerlessness of their poverty; their inability to influence events. It is a powerlessness not of their own making. Neither of these men have any less capacity than the other men around the table, the public servants and the business operators and us foreigners.

We have seen how much Dith and Thongkhan care for their community, how much time and effort they put into trying to improve living conditions in their village, how they each have individual skills that have not been nurtured or enabled simply through lack of money or through having no useful connections.

Its not smart or even useful, but my feeling is one of anger. Anger at the unfairness. Anger at the inequality. Anger that Thongkhan and Dith have to struggle against uneven odds while others wheel and deal.

So when I hear Chanthy ask again, 'Can I tell them now?' Iain and I both say, 'Yes'.

Chanthy tells them we have arranged for another contractor, who has a roller, to take over immediately their contract finishes.

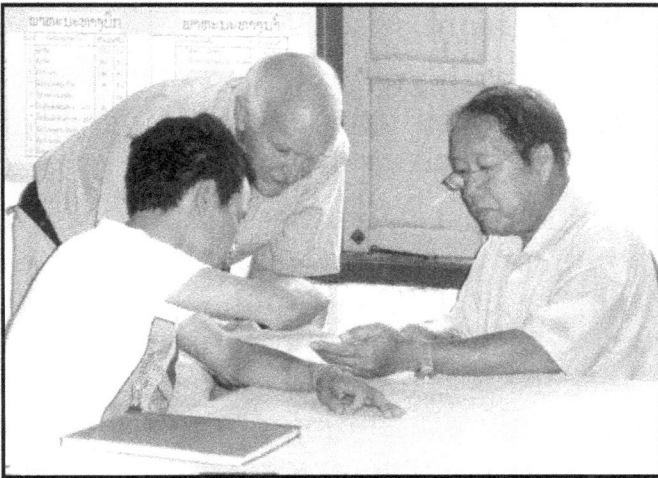

We explain that we have found a new contractor who has a roller and can finish the contract

We watch, with I admit to a degree of pleasure, as their jaws drop. Thongkhan and Mr. Dith smile at us and we mentally raise our thumbs in solidarity.

Animated conversation breaks out between the government people and Pimphone. I notice Thone, the Admin officer, remains somewhat aloof. I am now certain he had some inkling of our good news; perhaps through the other contractor.

Once the initial hubbub of surprise dies down Mr. Vijit asks for the name of the replacement company. We continue for a wee bit with the shadows and mirrors, but the game has lost its allure. It is Mr. Lea and his Muasone Road Construction Company, we tell them. It is quite apparent that everyone in the room knows Mr. Lea and of his company.

In one last throw of the dice Pimphone suggests, 'He will charge more.'

Iain confidently retorts, 'No. In fact he will charge less than you would have charged, ' and to rub it in, 'if you'd had a roller.'

The ball is most definitely in Pimphone's court. Vijit, Khamphou and Thone all look at him. He nods to himself, takes out his mobile phone and his cigarettes, gets up from the table and leaves the room. More tea is drunk and everyone chats among themselves while pretending not to try to overhear what Pimphone is saying outside into his mobile. Of course we can't understand what he's saying, but it's not rocket science to work out whom he is calling.

In less than five minutes he comes back, his relaxed manner and easy smile restored. It is all arranged. Mr. Phali's Khamluanglat Road Building Company has leased the roller from Mr. Lea's Muasone Road Building Company, together with a driver. The roller is leaving the dam worksite, more or less as we speak, on the back of a truck and will arrive in Muang Nam by mid-morning tomorrow. This means it will be taken on to NaLin where it will finish The Road in two days, by Saturday night, within the agreed time. It will of course cost the originally agreed price. Win some loose some, we thought. But everyone is happy.

That night we join several hundred other people in the grounds of the wat in Simougkoun village on the edge of Muang Nan for the opening alarums of *Boun Bung Fai*, the Rocket Festival. The proceedings are a somewhat dangerous mix of giant Roman Candles, filled with large amounts of highly inflammable phosphorus. These are carried by half a dozen men apiece on big bamboo platforms decorated with giant sprays of flowers and greenery among unrestrained, milling crowds out to have some crazy fun.

The first night of the Rocket Festival in Simougkoun village on the outskirts of Muang Nan

A long table is cheerfully manned by a dozen or so young novices selling tiny rolls of paper chosen at random by those wanting to know what their future holds. Other novices, scores of them, crowd the upper balcony of a highly ornamented wooden tower. Older monks, pouring out of the beautifully decorated wat at the end of a session of prayers and chanting, are busy taking photographs of each other and the seething masses.

Among these we come across Pimphone's truck drivers Saeng and Phuang who of course by now have heard about the drama over the roller. They grin like fellow conspirators. Sort of *workers of the world unite*.

And now a man is dashing up to one of the platforms brandishing a large burning taper. I feel Jai pulling gently at me from behind and making rain-falling gestures only it isn't rain he wants to protect me from but still-burning falling ash. The massive Roman Candle explodes into a huge skyward roaring jet, with great force; sparks and smoke and smell fill the air.

Some of the sparks fall and bounce off the wooden roofs of the wat and surrounding outbuildings including the one whose high top balcony is stuffed with novices hanging out as far as they can in order to get the best possible view of proceedings. Everyone spontaneously makes the universal sounds of appreciation for a splendid fire show. Ooooh....aaaah! as there are more lightings and fountains of exploding phosphorescence.

Friday May 24th, dawns and the main street of Muang Nan starts to come alive with utes and small trucks which are wildly dressed overall with forests of palm leaves and tropical flowers. But although we are disappointed that its arrival means we will have to forgo seeing the actual rocket-launching part of the Festival, we are hanging out for the first appearance of one particular and much more pedestrian vehicle, our highly anticipated and longed-for roller.

By nine o'clock Pimphone is pacing the roadside, ever-present mobile in hand. For the past half-hour or so he has been pressing the redial button and getting an update that he passes on to us via Chanthy. This is as stressed as we have ever seen a Lao become, though even then Pimphone still maintains his outward affability. It occurs to us that this whole schmozzle over the roller might have been cause for some, pardon the pun, Lao-level, angst between him and his company-owner brother.

The number of greenery bedecked vehicles increases. They are all moving, slowly so as to be all the more appreciated by onlookers, in the same direction, towards open fields at the edge of town. Men carrying lethal-looking super-sized handmade rockets saunter by accompanied by young children who are so bubbling with anticipation they cannot but skip and hop and run and laugh.

We yearn to join them, but these are the last couple of days of a two-and-a-half-year, demanding journey for us and I have my own version of skipping, hopping, running and laughing to do. I hope.

Pimphone announces the truck bearing the roller is just a few minutes away. We line the road, straining like ardent royalists to be the first to catch a glimpse of the creature to which we have attached all our deepest hopes. And there is it. What a beauty. A fat, crushingly bumptious, gorgeously yellow, beast of a machine. We wave and the driver of the truck carrying our redeemer laughs and waves back.

The replacement roller on its way to NaLin

We all cram into the back tray of Headman Dith's much abused vehicle and follow the laden truck, against the flow of Rocket Festival traffic, out of town and onto The Road To NaLin.

28

ROLLING THE ROAD and PHUJONG

Laos, like the majority of countries with basic rural economies and more or less non-existent infrastructure, has bypassed telephone landlines and gone straight to cheap, simple mobiles, so by now literally everyone in NaLin knows the machine is on its way and comes out to celebrate its arrival.

During the bumpy ride in we meet Mr. Keo the roller driver, an unusually taciturn man in his twenties who spends the entire journey fingering a cigarette he never lights and repeatedly sniffing on a strong-smelling nasal inhaler.

It is impossible not to notice Mr. Keo has a badly damaged, all but useless, left foot. This is perhaps due to a workplace accident, but in Laos, with its appalling rates of birthing injuries as well as deaths, it is just as likely something Keo has always endured and is more than enough to make his reticent manner understandable.

What I did not anticipate was Keo's dual personality. Once the roller is unloaded at the point on the track where it joins The Road into NaLin and Keo has limped to its side, he uses his strong upper body to pull himself up into the driving seat, manually hauling his damaged foot into a secure position behind his fully functioning leg. He then instantly becomes a different man, unimpeded by the damage to his body. Here he is in charge. Firing up his machine, he turns his cap backwards and with a warm grin and a wave takes off on his mission, all signs of his cool reserve completely banished.

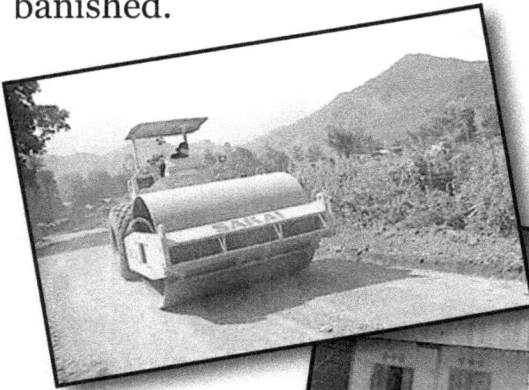

The new roller at work

Again it is the children who are most effervescent in their appreciation of this almost final act in the drama of The Road. The boys quickly work out that not only does the roller roll flat anything in its path but it also vibrates mightily.

I say almost the final act because there is one more piece of fun to be had: the water-tanker. This extremely battered piece of machinery had been used during the first week of operations on The Road but not since because there had been a few tension inducing, but thankfully brief, rainfalls. In fact these had actually been useful in helping to compact the topcoat.

Now another Mr. Phuang follows behind Keo, atop his big yellow Sakai roller and is trailed by laughing children enjoying a cooling spray in the immense heat of the day. On his next and subsequent runs through the village, Keo vibrates the dampened topsoil into a rain resistant thickened crust.

Pimphone is here of course, overseeing the completion of the job, soaking up the atmosphere and looking very relieved it is all coming to a happy ending.

Villagers stand in their doorways. Some of the open areas between houses are also flattened and given the heavy shake, rattle and roll treatment. Already some extra drainage ditches have been chopped out by hand. Headman Dith has even put piping through the channel in front of his place and tamped extra soil down on top to protect this overflow conduit.

Two women, mother and daughter would be a good guess and apparently with no man in the household, having just returned from working a full day in the fields, scramble to dig their own overflow channel to carry the anticipated, badly needed but still much feared, heavy monsoon rains, away from an area beside their place. Their neighbours come to assist.

The roller works into the night, in order to finish the work by the following afternoon deadline

Keo carries on working under the headlights of his big yellow roller until well after the tropical night's blanketing darkness falls. He keeps driving and vibrating his roller as long as possible to ensure the job can be finished on the following day.

In the Sisombuth house we find Khamphou, the Roads Inspector, who has come out on his motorbike from Muang Nan, to check on the roller's progress and is bubbling over with stories of the rocket launchings at the Festival, that from his account was a literally blazing success. Simougkoun villagers were the winners of this year's contest for Best Rocket and were awarded the most appreciated amount of two million kip, or around $240.

In another piece of good local news, NaLin School principal, Mr. Thand and his family have won a million kip, or about $120, in this Festival weekend's big national lottery.

Khamphou says he will return tomorrow to walk The Road with us so as to have our word on it being satisfactory. He will be joined by his government colleagues who will participate in the inspection and also in the planned basi.

Leaving them all to have their evening meal, Iain and I go out back to the ablutions area. This politic description glosses over the viscous mud surrounding the broken, wobbly concrete slab, slippery with green mould, beside an earth trench and a dribbling tap. There is a pail of water and a small plastic scoop.

This is the spot where I have shared in the nightly bathing routine of Sydney. His mother, Binh, rests him back on her turned up feet to keep him out of the muck as she ladles water over his small body. It is also the only place to get water for cooking in the equally simple cooking spot just inside the back door.

Across a few more difficult-to-negotiate slabs is the low ceilinged attap hut with its squat loo and another pail of water that sloshes whatever is deposited to somewhere beyond the village.

The Sisombuth's house is the farthest out, on the edge of the village, at a bend in The Road before it takes off through the paddy fields. We remove our headband torches and in the dark strip to our underwear, hanging our clothes and our small travel towels, over a conveniently close bush. We spoon some tepid water over each other and soap up. I even shampoo my hair.

Suddenly the air comes alive with tiny, flickering, dancing lights. Fireflies: scores of them. The light from the full moon, undiminished by any electrical competition, turns the little separating earthen walls of the paddy fields a soft silver and illuminates the tin roof of the distant small wat. It's a literally breathtaking scene.

As we dry and redress in our day's sweat stained clothes Iain mentions that making this area cleaner, safer, more accessible and altogether more pleasant would be quite simple and that he has been talking with Thongkhan and drawing up plans. I then realize that morning's casual visit to 'Bunnings' in Muang Nam had rather more intent to it. A row of big blue plastic lidded barrels on a raised ramp alongside the house is part of these future plans.

'Just as long as any schemes do nothing to detract from this glorious view,' I stipulate.

Following on from the next morning's obligatory fried eggs we leave the house by stepping out onto The Road. There to our delight we find children, of a variety of ages, playing up and down the firm surface of The Road with homemade toys all with wheels.

One lad drags behind him the battered skeleton of a two-wheeled trolley. Another has two wheels

attached to a stick. This he pushes up and down, chattering to himself, at the head no doubt of his invisible-to-us army.

Around the corner comes another small fellow pulling a block of wood with wheels attached. The wood has been scooped out to form a cradle in which lies an empty sauce bottle. A girl with a skipping rope is out and about already with two of her friends on dilapidated bicycles. They are all enjoying the newfound freedom of The Road.

Not just the children. Adults too. We record some vox pop interviews for our now-planned docco, asking people what they feel about The Road. Their responses, as translated by Chanthy, are all heartwarming.

The sales pitch cry of a meat-seller brings the women out of their homes. They cluster around the small ice chest he has tied to the pillion seat of his motorcycle as he dips his white-gloved hands in and pulls out bits of this and that, guts and cuts. It would be somewhat less of a worry if his multi-holed gloves were clean. The women bargain. The salesman assures Chanthy that with such a good road he will now be able to continue visiting the village during the wet season.

A woman peddler arrives carrying a small basket of ants' eggs. The eggs of red ants are a Lao specialty. Boiled up they resemble puffed wheat. She too comments on how The Road will ease accessibility.

We call in on the woodworking workshop of ex-Pathet Lao soldier Sengchan Sitanong. His is the only small business operating in the village that is not to do with rice farming. With the assistance of a couple of young village men he converts logs from the surrounding forests into doors with simple, but beautiful carved decorations.

His primitive workshop would give any medical professional or Australian Occupational Health and Safety official the horrors: so many accidents waiting to happen. Belts and pulleys, saws and jacks all of them in desperate need of repair or at least maintenance: everyone in thongs and no protective eyewear or masks. Turkeys, ducks, chickens and dogs underfoot.

Sengchan with one of his doors

A couple of men are busy loading a utility truck with a dozen or so of Sengchan's doors for delivery to a hardware and construction outlet in a town further south. The vehicle will not leave until it is dark because that gives a better chance of avoiding road blocks set up by police ostensibly to check paperwork, but in reality topping up their low salaries. Hard to feel anything but sympathy for them when you hear they are sometimes not paid for months on end.

Having The Road will make a deal of difference to Sengchan's business as it will now be able to operate year round.

But of course not everything is sweetness and light because that's not the way with life. Khamphou and his band of merry men arrive including Chief Administration Officer of Nan District Mr. Thone. They make it clear they want to walk over a section of The Road, which we all do and they give it their seal of approval bringing smiles all round. But we insist we also want to go further up the road to the Hmong village of Phujong.

This section of road, from the turn-in to NaLin on up into the mountain has been given a basic upgrade by the local government under Mr. Vijit. It was not a part of our original quest to include improvements to this track while building The Road to NaLin. But we feel a sense of moral obligation because we have on previous visits spoken in Vijit's office in Meung Nam with Phujong Headman Laisiew as well as Mr. Xienghom, headman of the Khmu village of Houayhe At this previous get together we told them that we still hoped in the future to do more with their road but that it was just not possible this time.

We don't want to leave town without re-visiting

their villages and telling them we will be back. Reluctantly the civil servants agree to accompany us on the drive up. En route Head of the Development Group at Khoktom, Mr. Boun Pheng, points out the fifteen or sixteen places where culverts are required. Each culvert and its installation will cost upwards of $1000 each. Just before Phujong the truck has to cross a small stream. In the wet season this becomes a dangerously fast flowing river making it often impossible for villagers to get in or out. Here a culvert bridge is required.

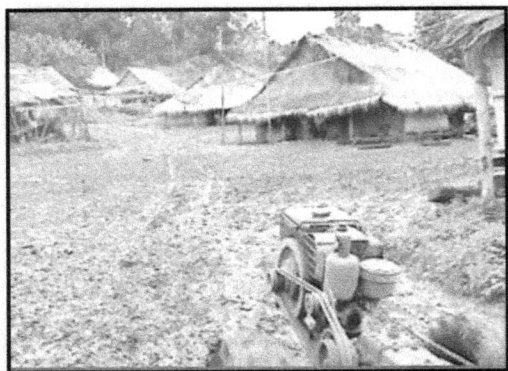

The Hmong village of Phujong is far poorer than NaLin

Phujong is as miserable a place as we remember it. The Lao Government's attitude to and treatment of its minority groups is a serious blot on their social contract with its people. In general the majority Lao Loum also carry varying degrees of personal prejudice against these people. This unacceptable aspect of Buddhism dismisses the country's believers in animism as lesser creatures.

There are about 260 people in Phujong, some are Yao, some are Khmu, but most are Hmong. They are members of a group who with their additional heavy historical baggage of assisting first the French, then the Americans, as guerrilla fighters in the two Indo-China wars in the sixties and seventies, are the most despised.

Headman Laisiew waits for us in his weather-beaten, earthen-floored hut. He looks strained and tired. Only Mr. Boun has the good manners to sit with him and explain how it is that NaLin has become the beneficiary of Australian aid while the people of Phujong will have to endure the squalid horrors of their connecting track for yet another wet season. Laisiew listens with grace.

Development Officer Boun Pheng explains to disappointed village Headman Laisiew why the new road work does not include Phujong

On the trip back down to NaLin village we stop to pick up a group of young Khmu girls from Houayhe who have been out in the forest collecting wild mushrooms. They are delighted to get a lift but when Mr. Thone attempts to buy some of their mushrooms the oldest girl, the leader of the pack, perhaps in her early teens, adamantly refuses. She insists her villagers, around 340 mostly Khmu people, need them for food; chattering and laughing they hop nimbly over the tailgate and disappear into the collection of   simple huts.

29

FAREWELL BASI

Our farewell basi is to be held in Headman Dith's home. Chanthy's Aunt, Thongmee Phonevilai, has as usual done an impeccable job in the creation of a large, ornately decorated *phakhoun* bedecked with flowers and many scores of white cotton wrist-ties. A large cooked and plucked chicken encircles the base. Scattered over the carcass are small packets of sweet and savoury nibblies.

The main room is filled with the happy faces of the many people who over the last two and a half years we have come to know and who have honoured us by sharing their lives with us.

The floor of the attached cooking space is crammed with women chopping and mixing. As a sign of respect they have put on their very best sinhs and blouses and draped their finest prayer scarves over their shoulders and across their hearts.

As always Mr. Thongdy Thongsamou, the former

monk, initiates the basi ceremony by beginning to chant blessings in formal Pali, a signal to everyone, even the most rambunctious of the multitude of children, to quieten down and join in the large roughly concentric circles of kneeling people who radiate out from the *phakhoum*. With bowed heads and hands placed together in a nop they open themselves to the mystery.

Thongdy is a consummate showman and knows how to grab and hold the throng's attention. He closes his eyes, appearing to go into a trance. The pace and sound level of his chanting goes up a few notches as he places his fingertips on the beaten metal plate on which the *phakhoum* stands. We follow the lead of Chanthy and his family and do the same. I feel the light touch of someone's fingertips on my shoulder and know that another person has placed their fingertips on that person's shoulder and so on right across the roomful of people. In this way, it is said the spirit power is transferred. A sensation of vibrating stillness crackles through the atmosphere.

At the point where the pulse of all the people in the room throbs as one beat and the pain in my knees has reached screaming point, Thongdy removes his fingertips from the plate, sits back on his heels and the thrilling moment subsides. He takes a single strand of cotton from the *phakhoum* and starts to stroke it continuously over the backs of Iain's hand then mine, all the while chanting an animist mantra as an invocation to the spirits of the netherworld to bring together the thirty-two khwans or guardians of one's soul.

Then, as if released, people immediately begin to talk in a heightened animated fashion, to each pull several cotton threads from the *phakhoum* and move in on us to begin the ritual tying of threads around our wrists that will capture, repair and sustain our souls.

With the entire room a hubbub of voices and our wrists thick with tied threads, we now begin to tie threads onto the wrists of others while murmuring our own high hopes for them. In the midst of all these happenings Iain, while sitting pressed back against a wall, is attempting to shoot some video with his camera held in one hand while the wrist is being tied with cotton and I am trying to take some stills. As a bottle of deadly lao-lao appears, Thongkhan offers to take some shots and I am happy to pass my camera over to him. Just the smell of the lao-lao makes my throat contract and my nose tickle, but Iain manages to swig a half glass and everyone laughs and cheers appreciatively.

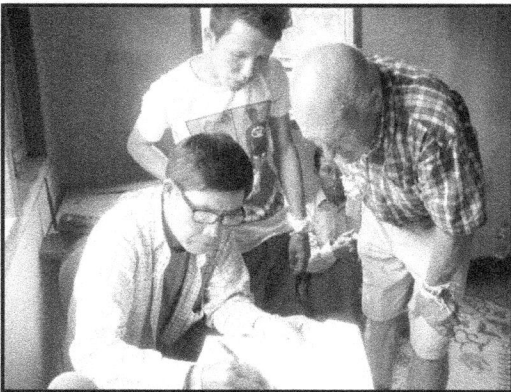

Final signatures on the documents

We take a brief break to sign the final papers and then lunch is served.

Long strips of plastic table-cloth are laid out on the floor

291

and many, many dishes of food are spread along them. Pimphone of course is here. His sense of relief at The Road being finished must come only a whisker short of ours. All the government men Khamphou Thongkammapon, Boun Pheng and even Mr. Thone are here as well as Mr. Laisiew and Mr. Xienghom from Phujong and Houayhe

We attempt to invite Chanthy's mother, Buachan Phonemanee, who looks graceful in her special occasion clothes, to come in from the kitchen area and join us with her son, but no amount of asking will persuade her.

In an atmosphere of great good humour, amongst animated conversation the food is rapidly consumed. The men go outside to smoke while the women start the process of clearing up. With this done they begin to drift away in the same way they came together; without ceremony, goodbyes or thank yous but with a great sense of camaraderie, having shared one more good time, accepting that life rolls on, bringing with it what it will. Good times, bad times, even a Road.

That evening, our last in the village and under the numinous light of a full moon, Iain and I walk The Road. The young girl child skips alongside us, something that she could not have done previously with any degree of ease on the old track.

Less than a week later the village of NaLin held yet another basi, this one for Party officials. An awning was set up to shade a section across the hard top of The Road and there they all are, in the photographs we receive shortly after returning home; all rather solemn-looking men, all wearing polished shoes, shirts and long trousers, sitting at a row of desks and chairs, obviously brought down from the primary school for this formal occasion. Chief Administration Officer of Nan District, Mr. Thone, is prominent among them. Someone has made name cards and put them in place. Behind them red, white and blue bunting is draped alongside the flag of Laos and yes, a poster photograph of the country's first Prime Minister.

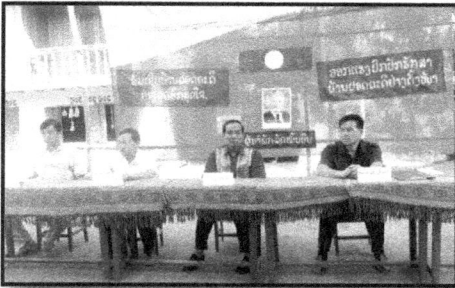

A Party for the Party. Government officials help celebrate The Road

But look, there are other photos and these show women, only women, squatting on their haunches outside one of villager's kitchens, chatting and laughing as they chop the meat for the laap. With the juxtaposition of these two shots Thongkhan, who took the photographs, tells the story.

Women prepare the feast

A few weeks after that, Chanthy sends us photographs of himself and his sister, taken at the graduation ceremonies at their college marking what they as a family have achieved; this boy and girl who had grown into a man and woman in the short time we have known them celebrate this achievement with their Mum and Dad. Thongkhan, Buachan, lee and Chanthy stand in the

Chanthy and his sister Bounlee

traditional posed shots, swamped in flowers. Each of them has the knowing look of people who are aware their lives have changed.

******

People can sit around discussing the pros and cons of international aid and how it corrupts both the giver and the receiver. They can cant on all they like about only giving aid to 'people who deserve it'.' Like if people 'need' aid don't they automatically 'deserve' it? They can attempt to justify a short arms and long pockets approach by pointing out that donated monies will be misused or lost in transit.

They can even ask whether giving is a form of patronizing and why are European countries still doing their good works in Asia, isn't that just an extension of colonialism? None of this sophistry holds any allure or traction with me anymore.

This book and Iain's documentary came about from our desire to share the story of The Road with the villagers of NaLin and with those who made it happen and to say a heartfelt thank you to you all.

Kopchai lai lai.

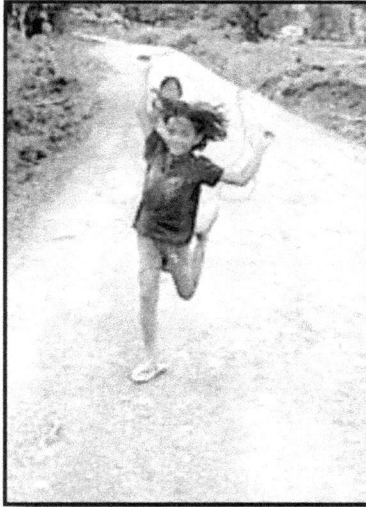

A small project... a world of difference.

POST SCRIPT

Of course it didn't just end there.

We hadn't planned on making a documentary film or writing a book. We had been so intent on getting The Road built that we hadn't looked any further ahead. So it came as something of a surprise when Iain's docco was generously given a free fund-raising screening at our local Cinemax theatre in Kingscliff, northern New South Wales; a screening which kick-started a whole new campaign:

> *The Road to Phujong...*
>
> *...taking the Road to NaLin a Step Further.*

In Laos, Chanthy was able to download the documentary from the Vimeo website and take his laptop down to NaLin where he set it up on a chair to show the villagers. They were all engrossed.

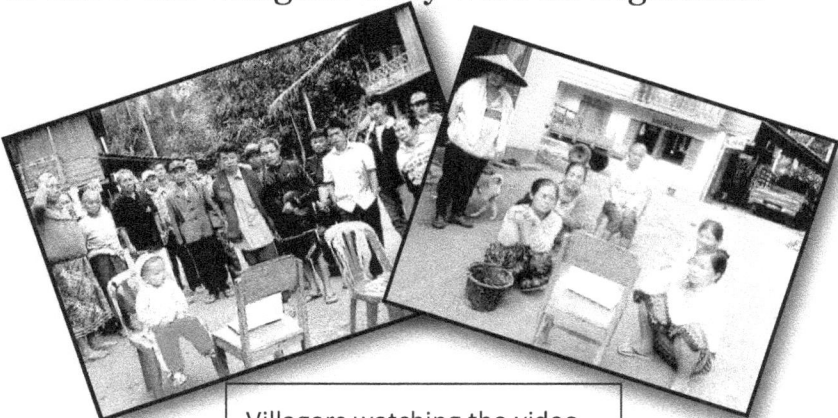

Villagers watching the video

A generous donation of $5000 by my Sydney gynaecologist and fertility expert, Dr. Anne Clark, was the psychological and financial impetus we needed to push on and do more.

Within a few months enough money had come in from new individual donations to return to Laos and oversee, much to the delight of the Hmong and Khmu villagers, the building of the sixteen essential culvert drains on the extended road between NaLin and the even more distressed Hmong village of Phujong.

The Australian Embassy in Vientiane, through its Direct Aid Programme administered by the then Ambassador Lynda Worthaisong, also kicked in $5000 and the new Ambassador John Williams was tickled pink to have an iconic kangaroo roadside sign, donated by our local Tweed Shire Council back home, placed at a road junction to mark their contribution.

Ambassador John Williams ...and the sign in place

This time the contractor was Kaisone Bolikhanhaexay, a culvert specialist whose rapidly expanding family company has earned its stripes by installing over a thousand culverts during the recent up-grading of National Route 4 between Luang Prabang and Xainyaburi. Sone and one of his ten-strong teams of extremely hardworking men plus an excavator and a couple of ten-tonne trucks, were able to get the huge job done in less than two weeks.

Culverts going in

First vehicle over a completed culvert

But what was even more pleasing was to see, on our return to NaLin, that The Road had stood up to the rigours of its first wet season without any signs of destruction. These *before and after* comparison shots of a few sections of the road, give some idea as to the improvement it has made in the lives of the villagers.

Before & After 1

Before & After 2

Before & After 3

Not only has The Road enabled the villagers much improved and easier access to the outside world for their produce, as well as for any

emergencies, but they can now get materials in to build and repair. We saw three houses under construction and were told their owners would not have even thought of starting under the conditions that existed before.

In addition, the two-day-long Boun Khong Khoa, Rice Harvest Festival, normally held in other villages in the district, was for the first time held in NaLin while we were there. And it was only made possible because of the quantum change in accessibility created by The Road to NaLin.

So now there is this book and of course another upcoming docco, plus ongoing plans. We are presently involved in establishing a Pilot Water Project to individual homes in NaLin.

And naturally there's always more that can be done, particularly, as we've said, in the more disadvantaged minority villages of Houayhe and Phujong, further along the road. And there's even another village, Nan Nouan, further out still, that we've never even visited, and which is apparently in need of aid... including a decent road.

So, as Iain mentioned early in the documentary film, it seems a bit like a road without end... but that's okay. Perhaps you'd care to join us.

View

THE ROAD TO NALIN

a 40-minute documentary

at: http://vimeo.com/74511058

or purchase through Amazon On Demand

DONATE TO THE ROAD TO NALIN FUND
COMMONWEALTH BANK OF AUSTRALIA
MURWILLUMBAH
NSW 2484
AUSTRALIA
BSB   062-580
ACCOUNT NUMBER   1029-7109

SWIFT CODE FOR DONORS FROM OUTSIDE
AUSTRALIA: CTBAAU2S

The Road to NaLin Fund is legally registered as
Charitable Fundraising Authority CFN/21888 with
the Government of New South Wales, Australia,
through Communities New South Wales.

Contact us direct on iaintrish@mac.com

ABOUT THE AUTHOR

TRISH CLARK has been a journalist all her working life, a period of over fifty years, in which she has worked as a newspaper columnist, a feature writer for major magazines and newspapers, a radio broadcaster and television reporter, as well as a producer of radio and television programs that have been broadcast nationally and internationally.

She helped establish and worked with the internationally successful science program for television, *Beyond 2000*, which was aired by the Discovery Channel for more than a decade.

In 2003/4 Trish spent 18 months working, with her husband, Iain Finlay on the Voice of Viet Nam Radio network, as Editors and Radio Programmers, while training local Vietnamese reporters in English usage, editing and on-air presentation techniques.

Trish is the author of eleven books, which include a biography, as well as fiction and non-fiction publications, five written jointly with her husband, Iain, on Africa, South America and the South Pacific, Viet Nam and Central Asia. She and Iain have children and grandchildren and when not traveling, live in Australia in the Tweed Valley, in northern New South Wales.

Read about other titles by Trish Clark:

CHILDREN OF BLINDNESS
AN IMMACULATE CONCEPTION
ANDREA
AUSTRALIAN ADVENTURERS
MOTHERHOOD

with **Iain Finlay**

GOOD MORNING HANOI
THE SILK TRAIN
AFRICA OVERLAND
SOUTH AMERICA OVERLAND
ACROSS THE SOUTH PACIFIC

Titles marked with an asterisk were originally
published under Trish's previous name,
Trish Sheppard.

CHILDREN OF BLINDNESS
A Brutal Exposé of Bigotry and Prejudice in Outback Australia
Trish Clark

Causing a storm of controversy on first publication, Children of Blindness, a powerful drama set in the small, fictional, but archetypal outback country town of Woongarra, depicts with stunning force, the violent interaction of a small group of people; black and white, over a period of little more than a week, in which three of them die.

Based on actual events at the time, this searing novel opens with Dougo Foster returning from six months in prison to find his children taken into care because of gross neglect by his drunken, pregnant wife, Flo. His attempts to get them back are the central thread along which the story unfolds, revealing layer upon layer of alcohol-fuelled degradation, violence and hopelessness for the indigenous community, amidst virtual total disapprobation and contempt from most of the white residents of the town. But fortunately not all.

And then there's the law; the compassionate cop, in contrast to his red-neck colleague, who regards all aborigines as hopeless bloody boongs. There is, however, little either can do when a series of events combine to tip the teetering township over the edge, into a night of unremitting horror.

(Available now in hard copy and eBook formats)

AN IMMACULATE CONCEPTION
Trish Clark

'...just when you thought it was safe to get on
with your own life.'

Cathy Connolly is revelling in the newfound joys of being Sam's grandmother. At work she is Ms. Catherine Stuart, a high-powered, senior executive in the Education Department. She's in good health, her husband Steve, is a successful architect, she has a happy daughter, a settled son and daughter-in-law, an erratic but charmingly likable brother and a distant, but well-loved mother.

Suddenly, within the space of less than two weeks, her life plunges into disarray. A colleague at work is trying to push her out of her job, Steve wants to take off in a 4-wheel drive for the Kimberleys, her daughter has given her boyfriend the boot, her brother wants to leave his wife and two daughters for a woman twenty-five years younger, and her son is donating his sperm to a lesbian couple. But, worst of all, Cathy finds she has cervical cancer.

'Life has taken a sudden lurch,' her voice was tremulous. 'Last week it all seemed so simple and straightforward. I feel as though I have stepped off into the deep end.'

'Just keep treading water and ring your Mum.' Steve told her.'

A fascinating and witty slice of modern Australian life, An Immaculate Conception highlights the dramatically changing standards, morals, and attitudes, not only of the cool, modish inhabitants of Sydney's eastern beach suburbs, where it is set, but of the whole country.

(Available now in hard copy and eBook formats)

A N D R E A
Trish Clark

Ahead of the kiss and tell pack by several decades *Andrea* was a close intimate of European royalty and silent-screen Hollywood stars as well as Australian politicians and socialites. She also spent four character-building years in a Japanese prisoner of war camp.

At the time of its publication her no-holds-barred biography caused a legal flurry at the highest levels. Despite demands for its publication to be banned, it has gone on to become an established social history of a time when live radio was the power domain and Andrea was its Queen. 'He was up me like a rat up a rope,' is just one of her earthy comments about an Australian Prime Minister.

Now, with all her personal papers stored in their own archive at the Library of NSW its time to re-read her story and be amazed how little has changed when it comes to Sex, Money and Politics.

(Digital version in production)

M O T H E R H O O D
Trish Clark

Fifteen women living through the various stages of motherhood from pregnancy to the anticipation of an empty nest, reveal their innermost desires and fears. While dealing with the unexpected blows of early widowhood, an offspring's physical incapacity, or even a child's death from drug addiction, they unveil the determination and courage that is at the core of their chosen lifelong role.

Strung along the thread of the author's own experiences their survival mantra, at a time when the choice for motherhood is no longer a natural given, is the feeling that there is only one thing worse than having children and that is not having them.

(Digital version in production)

AUSTRALIAN ADVENTURERS
Trish Clark

What drives a person to purposely place themselves beyond the comfortable, safe borders of the known; to push on further, to the risky edge and perhaps even over it?

Is there some intangible physic payment for placing yourself in physical jeopardy? Is that reward so addictive that it cannot be resisted as it grows to be a compulsion beyond family, friends, financial reward, even life itself.

Twenty *Australian Adventurers,* of all ages, share the passion that drives them to film sharks in the wild, climb Everest or become Australia's first aviatrix. To solo sail or to helicopter solo around the world. To voyage alone in the Antarctic or to recreate the 4000-kilometer open boat voyage of the Bounty mutineers. To be determined to hold the world hang gliding records for both height and distance at the same time, or to be the first to canoe right around the Australian continent. To put grandmotherhood on hold in order to become a backpacker, or to join the wartime resistance. Stories about those who dare ...to delight and challenge those who stay at home.

(Digital version in production)

T HE SILK TRAIN
Iain Finlay & Trish Clark

The Silk Train is travel adventure with a geo-political backbone. Veteran journalists Iain Finlay and Trish Clark set out to travel 21,000 kilometres from Singapore to Venice, by hopping on and off trains up through South East Asia, across China, Central Asia, the Caucasus, Turkey and the Balkans. Much of their route covers territory along which the ancient Silk Road trails wound their way over the past two thousand years. They planned to use rail lines that form part of an embryonic, UN-backed Trans-Asian Railway network, that will eventually create unbroken freight and passenger corridors all the way from China's far-eastern seaboard, to Europe.

While visiting some of the great historic sites of China and Central Asia, among them: Xi'an, Dunhaung, Samarkand and Bukhara, they also become aware of the changing dynamics of Big-Power politics across the vast Central Asian steppes, once the stamping grounds of Genghis Khan and Tamerlane, which now include the newly independent countries of Kazakhstan, Kyrgyzstan and Uzbekistan. They very quickly realise that, by far the most important items of trade along the modern equivalents of the Silk Road, are now oil and natural gas. Oil is the new silk. It is the new trans-national currency of the Silk Road, with China and its voracious, seemingly insatiable appetite for energy, emerging as the most significant factor in the political and economic arena of Central and South East Asia.

Further west, Russia's increased pressure on the Caucasus, particularly Georgia, is just another indication of how vital the world's dwindling energy resources are and will remain for most of the twenty-first century. By journey's end, in Venice, they realise they have travelled a very different Silk Road than that of Marco Polo.

(Illustrated hard copy version available now)

GOOD MORNING HANOI
Iain Finlay & Trish Clark

When Iain Finlay and Trish Clark arrive in Hanoi on a one-year work assignment for the English language service of the communist government-run radio network, they can hardly foresee the intense and exceptional experiences that await them. Coming to Vietnam for an Australian aid agency, their intended role is to coach and instruct, or at least to share their knowledge, with a small group of young reporters. But they find that they learn more than they teach.

As friendships with their colleagues grow, Iain and Trish are involved in developing and presenting a daily radio program - the first run by Westerners on a regular basis - and they become immersed in the stimulating life of one of Asia's most enchanting cities. In the process, they gain fascinating insights into Vietnamese society and culture, as well as a greater understanding and respect for the new Vietnam.

Good Morning Hanoi also illuminates the lives of a group of people dwelling in crowded conditions around a small courtyard in central Hanoi where Iain and Trish find a house to rent, and who become like an extended family living in the heart of the city.

In Good Morning Hanoi, Iain and Trish, two of the founders and producers of the international television program Beyond 2000, return to a country from which they had reported during the Vietnam War. They find an extraordinarily friendly people whose resilience and irrepressible good nature enable them to put the past behind them and move into the future with confidence.

(Illustrated hard copy version available now)

By Iain Finlay & Trish Clark
THREE INCREDIBLE ADVENTURES:

Africa Overland
South America Overland
Across the South Pacific

You'd love to travel to remote and exotic places but...you have kids. So? Why let that stop you? You're worried about their education...think you should wait. Don't!

Iain and Trish didn't. They made three big journeys through some of the toughest territories in Africa, North and South America and the South Pacific with their two young children. Using public transport; buses, trains, trucks, trading vessls, sometimes hitching, each of them shouldering their own backpack, they spent months at a time on the road.

Spread over period of just on four years, their travels took them first from Capetown to Cairo. Eighteen months later they journeyed overland from Canada to Tierra del Fuego, at the bottom tip of South America and within another year and a half, they island hopped across the South Pacific from Chile to Australia.

Not only did they survive to write these three books, which also look at the history, politics and way of life of the countries through which they traveled, but, with the passing of the years they know their travel adventures truly sealed an on-going adult friendship with their children.

(Read on)

AFRICA OVERLAND
Iain Finlay & Trish Clark

Capetown to Cairo! A magical phrase...the journey of a lifetime. Around 12,000 kilometers, nine countries, four months on the road with nothing booked or arranged in advance. With their two children; a son aged eight and daughter nine, carrying their own back-packs and often sleeping in rough circumstances (like in the back of a truck laden with copper ingots), Iain, Trish and the kids get to see: Kruger National Park, Victoria Falls and travel on the TanZam railway. They experience the vast herds of game in Serengetti, Lake Manyara,Ngorongoro Crater and Amboseli, go to the source of the Blue Nile in Ethiopia, travel on 'Kitchener's Railway' across the Nubian Desert from Khartoum to Wadi Halfa, Aswan and the great temples of the Nile Valley... all the way down to Cairo and the Pyramids.

(Illustrated digital version in production)

SOUTH AMERICA OVERLAND
by Iain Finlay & Trish Clark

This incredible journey includes much more than just South America. It starts in Canada as Iain, Trish, their ten-year-old son and daughter, aged eleven, set out in a blizzard that covers most of the US, to deliver a car cross-country to San Diego. Then they travel by train and bus through Mexico, Belize, Guatamala, El Salvador, Honduras, Nicaragua and Costa Rica to Panama. Along the way they visit the great Aztec and Mayan temples of Tenochtitlan, Palenque, Tikal and many others.

Then on to Ecuador and Peru, where they puzzle over the mysterious lines in the Nazca Desert and visit the fabled Lost City of the Incas at Machu Picchu. Across the Andes, on the Amazon headwaters, at Pucallpa and down-river, they find barges, ferryboats and a trading boat for a 3,000-kilometer, month-long journey down the Amazon to Iquitos and Manaus.

On through the Matto Grosso to Bazilia, Rio and Sao Paulo, Iguasu Falls, Montevideo and Buenos Aires, before hitching for much of the way south through Patagonia to the amazing glaciers of southern Argentina, the Magellan Straits and Tierra del Fuego. Here they reach the southernmost city in the world, Ushuaia,   Six months, 17 countries, 23,000 kilometers:

(Illustrated digital version in production)

ACROSS THE SOUTH PACIFIC
by Iain Finlay & Trish Clark

Leaving Santiago, Chile after a frightening night of earth tremors, Iain, Trish and their two children, now 12 and 13 years old, fly to Easter Island, where, using their own tents, they camp out in remote corners of the island as they explore the huge, enigmatic stone monoliths. From there, its Tahiti and the stunning beauty of Bora Bora, Morea and the unbelievable Tuamotu atolls. In the Cook Islands they board a copra trading vessel for a journey through the island chain; Aitutaki, Rakahanga and Manihiki. When it breaks down, mid-ocean, they go overboard with the crew to swim in water 3,000 metres deep. American and Western Samoa are next, in the midst of a typhoon. Then the pleasures and beauty of Tonga, the Fiji Islands, Vanuatu and New Caledonia, before finally returning to their home in Australia.

(Illustrated digital version in production)

HIGHADVENTUREPUBLISHING.COM
AND
HIGHADVENTUREPRODUCTIONS.COM
ARE PART OF
High Adventure Productions
PO Box 111
Tumbulgum, NSW 2490
EMAIL: IAINTRISH@MAC.COM
AUSTRALIA

www.ingramcontent.com/pod-product-compliance
Lightning Source LLC
Chambersburg PA
CBHW022329280326
41934CB00006B/585